Lionhead Rabbits

The moral rights of the author has been asserted
British Library Cataloguing in Publication Data
A catalogue record for this book is available from the British Library

ISBN 978-1-909820-01-2

Disclaimer and Legal Notice

Lionhead Rabbits

The Complete Owner's Guide to Lionhead Bunnies

The Facts on How to Care for these Beautiful Pets, including Breeding, Lifespan, Personality, Health, Temperament and Diet

Foreword

Hello and thank you for buying my book.

I hope that this book will provide a straightforward and practical guide giving you the information that you need to help you care for your Lionhead Rabbit.

Included in this book is information about Lionhead Rabbit care, habitat, cages, enclosures, diet, facts, set up, food, names, pictures, life span, breeding, feeding, a care sheet and costs.

I have written this book using American spelling as that is what I'm used to. I have given measurements in both feet and inches/pounds and ounces and also in metric. I have also given costs in US$ and GBP. Both the measurements and costs are approximate guides. I have done my best to ensure the accuracy of the information in this book as at the time of publication.

I trust that after reading this book you will feel more confident about owning and looking after a Lionhead Rabbit and that you have a wonderful time enjoying the pleasure they bring in the years to come!

All good wishes, Ann L. Fletcher

Acknowledgements

I could not have written this book without the help of my father. As one of five children growing up on the family farm, I cherished the moments I spent with my father taking care of his show rabbits.

After my father passed, I adopted his prized rabbits as my own. It was at a rabbit show that I was first introduced to the Lionhead Rabbit breed. It was love at first sight – I started breeding and showing them myself, sharing that joy with my own children, Mark and Stacey, through researching and writing this book.

I would also like to thank my wonderful husband John who has always been supportive of my hobbies and interests.

Table of Contents

Chapter One: Introduction

The Lionhead Rabbit is known for its long, wooly mane which is reminiscent of a regal male lion. These rabbits are newly domesticated, having been first recognized by the UK British Rabbit Council in 2002. Not only are these rabbits very attractive, but they are also extremely friendly and well-mannered. The Lionhead Rabbit makes an excellent pet for owners of all ages.

Lionhead Rabbits come in a variety of colors and patterns. What makes them unique, however, is the variety of mane types they exhibit. These rabbits have either a single or double mane depending on their genetics. Single-maned rabbits have a thin, wispy mane that diminishes with age. Double-maned rabbits, however, have a thick ring of hair around the head and body offset by shorter hair on the back.

Because they are a fairly new breed, Lionhead Rabbits are not yet common as household pets. Though they may be less common than other breeds, they are still an excellent choice for children, individual owners and families. If you have ever thought about buying a Lionhead Rabbit, or if you are already an owner and simply want to know more about caring for these animals, this book is just what you need to be successful.

In this book you will find all the information you ever wanted to know about the Lionhead Rabbit including facts about the breed, the breed's history and information regarding the care of these wonderful creatures. If you are a new rabbit owner, you will also find helpful tips for finding a Lionhead Rabbit breeder, picking out a healthy rabbit and setting up your rabbit's cage for the first time. After reading this book you will be equipped with extensive knowledge to help you properly care for your Lionhead Rabbits.

Glossary of Terms to Know:

Buck = an intact (unneutered) male rabbit

Dam = the mother rabbit

Doe = a female rabbit

Fostering = using a Doe rabbit other than the Dam to nurse one or more kits

Kindling = the process through which a Doe gives birth to a litter of kits

Kits = baby rabbits

Litter = group of baby rabbits birthed by a single mother

Sire = the father of a rabbit

Weaning = the process through which juvenile rabbits become independent from their Dam for food (they no longer suckle)

Chapter Two: Understanding Lionhead Rabbits

Lionhead Rabbits are a fairly new breed of domestic rabbit. The breed is recognized by the British Rabbit Council and by the American Rabbit Breeders Association (ARBA) as of February 1, 2014.

1.) What Are Lionhead Rabbits?

What makes these rabbits unique from other breeds is their long fur and wooly mane which was achieved by crossbreeding two different types of rabbits. The Lionhead Rabbit can be considered a dwarf breed because it remains fairly small, even in adulthood. This breed is popular as a family pet due to their gentle temperament and they are also bred and kept for show. These rabbits may exhibit two different mane types and they come in a variety of colors and patterns. In fact, it is possible for a single litter of Lionhead Rabbit babies to exhibit completely different colors.

Not only are these rabbits a unique and interesting breed, but they are also a joy to keep as pets. Lionhead Rabbits are naturally friendly and, if you spend plenty of time talking to them and handling them, they will get used to being around people. It is also important to remember that rabbits are social animals so, in addition to requiring plenty of affection, they also do well when kept with another rabbit for companionship.

2.) Facts About Lionhead Rabbits

The British Rabbit Council identifies the Lionhead Rabbit as a Fancy Breed. This puts these rabbits in the same class as other breeds like Angora, Harlequin, Himalayan and Netherland Dwarf rabbits. These rabbits are technically a cross between the Belgian dwarf and the miniature Swiss Fox – the breed was discovered in attempts to create a long-coated dwarf rabbit breed. Though this cross is largely accepted as the origin of the breed, there are reports that

Lionhead Rabbits were achieved through a crossing of Netherland Dwarf and Jersey Wooly rabbits.

Though the Lionhead Rabbit breed was discovered somewhat by accident, the breed became popular. In fact, this breed became more popular than the long-coated dwarf rabbit breeders were trying to achieve. As a result, breeders began to breed rabbits intentionally to achieve the long coat and mane of what is now recognized as the Lionhead Rabbit.

Lionhead Rabbits remain small, generally achieving a weight between 2 ½ and 3 ¾ lbs. (1.13 to 1.7 kg.). The bodies of these rabbits are fairly small and compact since they were bred from dwarf breeds. Though their bodies are small, the wooly coats and manes of this breed make them appear much larger than they actually are. Lionhead Rabbits typically exhibit a long, wooly mane around the head and neck that resembles the mane of a male lion.

The mane is typically 2 inches (5.08 cm.) long at minimum and it forms a circle all the way around the head. Some specimens of the breed have longer hair on the chest and face while some exhibit a V-shaped extension of the mane along the neck and back. Many specimens of the breed also exhibit a fringe of hair growing between the ears like a cap. The ears themselves grow to about 3 inches (7 .62 cm.) long.

Depending on the genetics of any given specimen, Lionhead Rabbits may be single or double-maned. These rabbits have a single mane when they receive 1 mane gene from the parents and a double mane when they receive 2 mane genes. The genotype of a single-maned Lionhead is Mm while the genotype of a double-maned rabbit is MM. Double-maned rabbits can be achieved through breeding two single-maned Lionheads or two double-maned rabbits.

Single-maned Lionhead Rabbits have a long, wooly mane around the head, including the ears and chin – the mane may also extend partially into the chest area. The mane in these rabbits is somewhat wispy and thin. As single-maned rabbits age, their mane may thin – it may also disappear in the summer and grow back in the winter months. Double-maned rabbits exhibit the traditional mane around the head as well as a ring of thick, wooly hair around the body. This extra mane is sometimes referred to as a "skirt".

Lionhead Rabbits have small bodies and bold heads. According to the breed standard as published by the British Rabbit Council, the body should be short and well-rounded with a broad chest. The hindquarters should be deep and firm to the touch. Lionhead Rabbits should have wide-set eyes and a well-developed muzzle. The ears should be upright and should not exceed 7.5 cm (2.95 inches) in length. They should be covered in fur but not to the extent of the Angora Rabbit breed.

The coat of this breed should be between 2 and 3 inches (5.08 to 7.62 cm.) in length, falling into a natural fringe around the rabbit's head. The fur should also be slightly longer on the chest, forming a sort of bib. Lionhead Rabbits have dense coats that roll back with slightly longer fur on the legs and flank in younger rabbits.

All recognized colors and patterns are accepted. It may be considered a fault by the British Rabbit Council if the fur on the flanks is too long, if the head is narrow or if the body or ears are too long. Lack of mane is grounds for disqualification from show as is a weight over 3 lbs. (1.36 kg.).

Summary of Lionhead Rabbit Facts

Breed Type: Fancy breed

Size: Dwarf

Weight: no more than 3 lbs. (1.36 kg.)

Ears: no more than 7.5 cm (2.95 inches) long

Eyes: widely spaced, bold and bright

Mane: 2 to 3 inches (5.08 to 7.62 cm.) in length, wooly

Coat: dense and medium length, rolling back over the body; may be longer on the chest

Color: all recognized colors are acceptable

Pattern: all recognized patterns are acceptable

3.) History of Lionhead Rabbits as Pets

The exact origins of the Lionhead Rabbit breed are unknown but the most commonly accepted theory is that they originated in Belgium. According to popular belief, the Lionhead Rabbit was the result of crossbreeding between a Swiss Fox rabbit and a Belgian Dwarf rabbit. Jersey Wooly and Dwarf Angora rabbits may have also been introduced into the bloodline at some point.

After the breed was initially created, it was then imported to the UK where individual breeders continued to develop the breed by crossbreeding it with other small breed and wooly rabbits. The Lionhead Rabbit breed is one of the first mutations of the domestic rabbit that has gained recognition since the 1900s. Perhaps this is the reason why its introduction to the United States and other countries outside of Europe was so slow. The Lionhead Rabbit breed wasn't introduced into the U.S. until 1999. That same year, the breed was discussed at a Breed Standards Committee meeting and a year later a working standard was agreed upon.

The Lionhead Rabbit was officially recognized as a breed by the British Rabbit Council in 2002 in the United Kingdom. It took some time, however, for the breed to be recognized in the U.S. with Arden Wetzel being credited with making the first attempt to get the breed recognized in

2004. Wetzel's attempt failed, so the breed was noted as "Certificate of Development" status with the American Rabbit Breeders Association (ARBA). In order for the breed to achieve recognition, three successful presentations must be made to the ARBA within a five-year span. The American Rabbit Breeders Association (ARBA) finally recognized the breed as of February 1, 2014.

a.) History of the British Rabbit Council

The breeding and showing of rabbits began over two hundred years ago. Throughout the nineteenth century, fanciers gathered to form local clubs for showing and improving individual breeds. The number of rabbit breeds recognized increased throughout the 1800s and early 1900s but by 1918, the most popular breed by far was the Beveren. In May of 1918 breeders of Beveren rabbits gathered to form a national club called The Beveren Club.

The Beveren Club served to raise the profile of rabbit breeding, adopting and standardizing new breeds. Eventually, the name of the club changed to the British Fur Rabbit Society and then to the British Rabbit Society. By 1928, over a dozen different breeds were recognized and interest in rabbit breeding began to grow. As a result, a new club was formed called the National Rabbit Council of Great Britain. The club grew quickly but conflicts arose between the two clubs which led to them eventually merging in 1934 to form the British Rabbit Council.

b.) History of the American Rabbit Breeders Association

The American Rabbit Breeders Association (ARBA) was founded in 1910 and has its headquarters in Bloomington, Illinois. The purpose of this association is to promote rabbit fancy and to facilitate commercial rabbit production. The ARBA is responsible for setting breed standards and sanctioning rabbit shows throughout North America. In addition to sponsoring local clubs and fairs, the ARBA holds a national convention show annually, drawing rabbit fanciers from around the globe.

Not only does the ARBA set breed standards and organize shows, it also serves to provide rabbit raising education. Every five years the ARBA publishes a detailed guide for rabbit fanciers called *Standard of Perfection*. The ARBA also publishes educational materials like guidebooks and posters including photographs of all the recognized rabbit breeds. Additionally, the ARBA has a library of over 10,000 books and writings on domestic rabbits – the largest single repository of its kind.

4.) Types of Lionhead Rabbits

The Lionhead Rabbit is a breed of domestic rabbit. The term domestic rabbit typically applies to several varieties of European rabbit which have been domesticated. The domestic rabbit belongs to the genus Oryctolagus in the family Leporidae. The species name of the domesticated rabbit is *Oryctolagus cuniculus*. All Lionhead Rabbits belong to the same species; they are simply one of over 50 unique breeds. This being the case, there are no genetic differences in "types" of Lionhead Rabbits aside from the genetics determining mane length, fur color and pattern.

Single-Maned Lionhead Rabbits

Whether a Lionhead Rabbit has a single or double mane is dependent upon its genetics. A single-maned rabbit receives only one gene for a mane – its genotype is Mm. Immature single-maned rabbits typically exhibit a well formed mane around the head with little wool on the rest of the body. As the rabbit matures, however, the mane may thin out.

Double-Maned Lionhead Rabbits

A double-maned rabbit receives two genes for a mane from its parents, making its genotype MM. These rabbits have a thick mane around the head as well as excess wool on the rest of the body. This wool should be less than 2 inches (5.08 cm.) and it should be longest on the sides, hips and butt. In order for double-maned rabbits to meet the breed standard, there has to be a clear break between the mane around the neck and the wool on the rest of the body – this break typically occurs just above the rabbit's foreleg.

Male Lionhead Rabbits

A male Lionhead Rabbit, or any breed of rabbit, is called a Buck. Many rabbit fanciers suggest that male rabbits tend to be gentler and more evenly tempered than females but, in general, Lionhead Rabbits are a friendly breed. Telling male from female rabbits can be difficult, especially while they are young. Both male and female rabbits have a "vent" that covers the genitals. By placing the rabbit on its back and gently pressing down just above the vent you can expose the rabbit's genitals to determine its sex. Juvenile male rabbits will have a small penis and, in mature males, the penis will be more developed.

Female Lionhead Rabbits

A female rabbit is called a Doe. Sexing a female Lionhead Rabbit can be done following the procedure described above. Pressing down on the skin above the vent will expose the vulva of the female rabbit – this looks like a rounded raised area with a slit running down the middle. Once a female rabbit reaches breeding age, the color of the vulva will change from pale pink to a deeper pink or red. Both males and females have two scent glands – one on either side of the genitals.

Baby Lionhead Rabbits

When baby rabbits are born, they are almost completely hairless and their eyes are closed. The mother will care for the babies for several weeks, protecting them from exposure and feeding them. By the tenth day after birth, baby rabbits usually open their eyes and their fur is generally developed enough to allow them to leave the nest safely. Weaning is best done by the age of 6 weeks, though it can be done as early as 4 weeks. It is unwise to keep baby rabbits with their mother past 3 months of age.

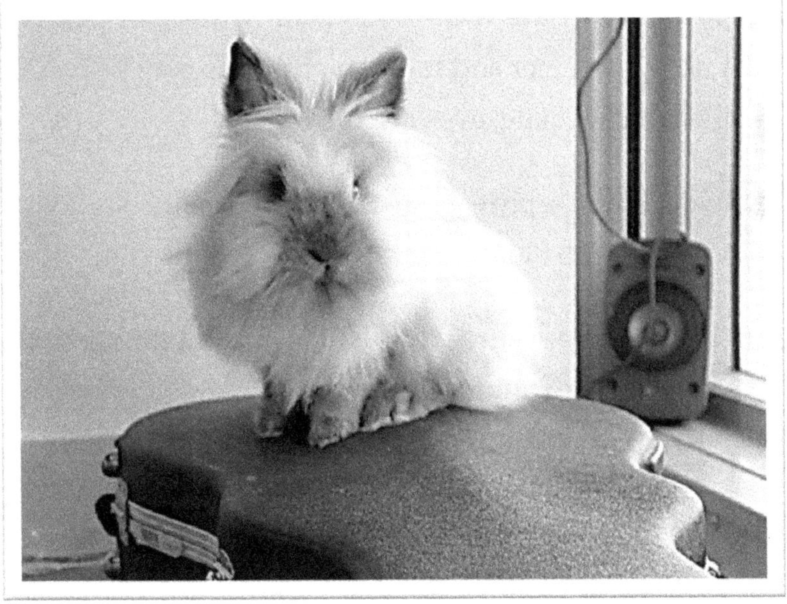

5.) Colors of Lionhead Rabbits

According to the breed standards, all colors and patterns are acceptable in Lionhead Rabbits. Some of the most common colorations include:

Sable Point = under color white, body color is brown; sepia brown color markings on the nose, feet, ears, legs and tail; eyes are brown

Black = rich, black fur all over the rabbit – may be darker on the face, ears and feet; eyes are typically brown

Pointed White = pure white body color with color points on the nose, ears, feet and tail – color points may be black, blue, lilac or chocolate; eyes are ruby

Blue Eyed White = pure white color uniform throughout the body; eyes are blue

Ruby Eyed White = pure white color uniform throughout the body; eyes are ruby

Chocolate = undercoat is dove gray, surface color is rich, dark brown over the entire body; eyes are brown

Tort = surface of the body is rusty orange in color with gray-black blended in on the sides, belly, head, rump, feet and tail; rust color extends well down the hair shaft, fading to off-white; eyes are brown

Chestnut = undercoat is dark slate blue with an intermediate band of orange; surface color is light brown with black ticking; under color of the belly is slate blue; eyes are brown

Blue = under color is light blue with surface color of dark blue extending well down the hair shaft; eyes are grey-blue

Broken = overall body color is white; color patches covering 10% to 50% of the body; eye color varies

Vienna = may be any color with a white blaze on the head; some rabbits have white paws or a white ring around the neck; eyes are blue

Lilac = under color is pale dove grey; surface color is dove gray with a pinkish tint; eyes are grey-blue

Chapter Three: What to Know Before You Buy

If you plan to keep exotic pets, you should always do your homework to determine whether or not you need a license to legally own them.

You may not think of a rabbit as an exotic pet, but there is a great deal of legislation in place to prevent improper selling and breeding of these animals.

1.) Do You Need a License?

Licensing requirements may vary from one country to another – even from one state to another – so it is wise to familiarize yourself with your region's regulations before you buy a Lionhead Rabbit.

a.) Licensing in the U.S.A.

In the United States, licensing requirements for pet rabbits vary depending on the intended use for the rabbits. Rabbit breeders, wholesalers and exhibitors must be licensed but retail pet store owners do not. These regulations are set forth by the Animal Welfare Act in order to ensure "proper animal care and comfort". There is no federal regulation stating that individuals keeping pet rabbits as part of a private collection need to have a license.

Though there are no federal laws requiring rabbit owners to be licensed, certain states do require rabbit owners to obtain a license – it all depends on how the state identifies the rabbit. Some states identify rabbits as livestock and thus regulate the number an individual can keep, while others identify them as pets. In Minnesota, for example, rabbits are considered pets and owners must pay $15 per year to license a rabbit if the animal is spayed or neutered. If the rabbit is not spayed or neutered, the annual fee is higher.

To find out whether your region requires a license to keep Lionhead Rabbits, contact your local council.

b.) Licensing in the U.K.

In the U.K. a license is not required to keep or breed rabbits. If you plan to import or export the rabbits, however, that is another matter and you may need to look into licensing requirements. If you plan to keep Lionhead Rabbits only as pets you will not need to obtain a special permit.

c.) Licensing Elsewhere

You may be surprised to hear that pet rabbits are prohibited in Queensland, Australia. Rabbits are not native to Queensland and are thus considered an introduced animal pest, threatening the survival of endangered native species and causing millions of dollars in damage each year. In Queensland, pet rabbits are declared as a Class 2 pest animal by the Land Protection (Pest and Stock Route Managements) Act of 2002. According to this act, it is illegal to introduce, keep or supply these animals without a proper permit.

It is not possible to obtain a permit to keep pet rabbits in Queensland for private purposes. The only situations in which a rabbit license may be issued are for certain types of entertainment (like magic shows) and for scientific purposes. The maximum penalty for keeping a rabbit without a license is $44,000. You will never see a rabbit for sale in a local pet store in Queensland.

2.) How Many Should You Buy?

Lionhead Rabbits are incredibly friendly and they generally prefer to be kept in pairs rather than being kept on their own. This is true of most rabbit breeds but it will depend on the personality of any individual rabbit. If you have never owned a rabbit before, you may want to start out with just one Lionhead Rabbit or adopt a pair that has already bonded. If you feel up to the challenge or are an experienced rabbit owner, your rabbits will enjoy being kept in pairs or trios rather than being left on their own.

****Note:** If you plan to keep your Lionhead Rabbits in an outdoor hutch, it is highly recommended that you keep two or more rabbits together. Indoors, a single rabbit is more likely to get adequate attention but outdoor rabbits require companionship if they are to have a happy life.

3.) Can Lionhead Rabbits be kept with Other Pets?

Because Lionhead Rabbits are such a friendly breed, they can be kept with certain other household pets – as long as you take certain safety precautions. Rabbits can generally be kept with cats and dogs, as long as their interaction is supervised and the rabbit does not show signs of fear. If your rabbit is hiding in his cage every time the dog or cat comes around, you may need to consider moving the cage to a place where your rabbit will feel more secure.

Be especially careful when letting your rabbit out of the cage around other pets because even well-trained dogs can be tempted by the quick movements of a rabbit. My best advice is not to take any chances but ultimately you must make a judgment call as you are best placed to know the character of your pets.

You should also be careful about keeping rabbits in the same house as certain noisy pets like birds. Rabbits have very sensitive ears and a vocal bird like a parrot could irritate your rabbit's ears. Ferrets are another pet that are not compatible with rabbits. Because ferrets are predators by nature they have the potential to seriously injure your Lionhead Rabbit. Aquarium fish and other pets kept exclusively in tanks can be compatible with rabbits as long as you keep the rabbit from chewing on any exposed electrical cords!

****Note**: If you plan to let your rabbit roam freely outside the cage, be sure to keep him from getting into other pets' foods.

4.) Ease and Cost of Care

Keeping Lionhead Rabbits as pets is an enjoyable experience, but it is also a responsibility. As a pet owner, you are responsible for providing your rabbits with all of the care they require. This includes food, shelter and veterinary care. All of these costs add up over time and, if you aren't prepared for them, they can become an issue. Before you purchase a Lionhead Rabbit, take the time to familiarize yourself with the kinds of costs you will need to cover in keeping these pets.

a.) Initial Costs

The initial costs of keeping Lionhead Rabbits include those costs which are required to purchase and prepare your rabbits' cage. Also included are the cost of the rabbit itself and any initial veterinary costs for spaying/neutering and vaccinations. Below you will find a list of initial costs as well as explanations of each:

Purchase Price: The price of Lionhead Rabbits varies according to where you purchase them. If you purchase your rabbit from a pet store or a private breeder you can expect to pay about $30 (£19.50). Another option is to adopt your rabbit from a local shelter – this option may save you some money and your rabbit may also be spayed or neutered.

Spay/Neuter: If you do not plan to breed your Lionhead Rabbits, it is a good idea to have them spayed/neutered to prevent unwanted breeding. The cost for this type of surgery is generally around $100 (£65), though you may be able to get it done for a lower price at your local veterinary clinic.

Microchipping: Having your rabbit microchipped is not a requirement, but it is always a good idea. A microchip is a tiny implant that can be inserted under your rabbit's skin and used to find and identify your rabbit if it gets lost. This service typically costs about $30 (£19.50).

Vaccinations: Before you introduce a new Lionhead Rabbit to your other rabbits it is wise to have it checked out by a veterinarian and updated on its vaccinations. The cost of this service may vary according to the vet you use, but the average cost is $50 (£32.50).

Cage or Pen: One of the most important initial costs for Lionhead Rabbits is the cage. This breed remains fairly small, so you will not need a large cage. You should, however, provide plenty of space for your rabbits to move around the cage – you may also want to provide an indoor or outdoor exercise pen. The initial cost for these items may vary but you should be prepared to spend as much as $300 (£195).

Cage Accessories: In addition to the cage itself, your Lionhead Rabbits will need a water bottle, food bowls, toys and bedding. You may also want to buy a travel carrier to use when you need to take your rabbits to the vet. Costs for these items vary but you should expect to spend about $100 (£65).

Other Tools and Equipment: Aside from your rabbit's cage and the initial costs of purchasing, neutering and vaccinating your rabbit you may also need to buy some tools and equipment. These tools, for the most part, should last you for several years – perhaps even the duration of your rabbit's life.

One example of something you might need is a litter pan – this is especially important if you plan to litter train your rabbit. You should also purchase basic grooming supplies including nail trimmers, brushes and grooming rakes. It would also be a good idea to buy separate sponges and brushes to use only when cleaning your rabbit's cage. The total cost for these additional tools and supplies will probably be close to $100 (£65).

Your Lionhead Rabbit is going to be part of your family and will require a lot of love and attention. The cost of keeping your pet has to be weighed up against the tremendous enjoyment and pleasure he or she will bring to your life. It might be worth considering having two as the initial cost is not that much more!

<u>Summary of Initial Costs:</u>

Cost Type	One Rabbit	Two Rabbits
Purchase Price	$30 (£19.50)	$60 (£39)
Spay/Neuter	$100 (£65)	$200 (£130)
Microchipping	$30 (£19.50)	$60 (£39)
Vaccinations	$50 (£32.50)	$100 (£65)
Cage or Pen	$300 (£195)	$300 (£195)
Cage Accessories	$100 (£65)	$100 (£65)
Other Tools/Equipment	$100 (£65)	$100 (£65)
Total:	$710 (£461.50)	$920 (£598)

b.) Monthly Costs

In addition to the initial costs explained above, you should also be prepared to cover certain recurring costs on a monthly basis. These costs include purchasing food and bedding for your Lionhead Rabbits in addition to providing routine veterinary care and replacements for toys and other cage accessories as needed. Below you will find a more detailed explanation of these costs:

Food: The amount of food you purchase each month will depend on the number of rabbits you keep. Some of the foods you will need to purchase include hay, greens or other vegetables and rabbit pellets. The average monthly cost to feed a Lionhead Rabbit is about $30 (£19.50).

Bedding: Again, the type of bedding you choose for your rabbit cage will determine the monthly cost. If you use newspaper as the bedding in your cage, you may not have to pay for it at all. Be careful, however, that you do not use colored magazines because these may contain toxins harmful to your rabbit. If you use hay, however, it could cost you up to $50 (£32.50) per month.

Veterinary Care: You may not need to take your rabbits to the vet every month but you should be prepared to cover the cost of unexpected veterinary visits. These may include emergencies and additional vaccinations. This shouldn't cost you more than $50 (£32.50) per year which is less than $5 (£3.25) per month, but of course this cannot be predicted and will depend on where you live.

Additional Costs: In addition to these monthly costs, you should also make room in your budget to cover unexpected costs. These may include the cost of replacement toys and food dishes as well as repairs to the cage. The total yearly average for these costs may be as little as $24 (£15.60) which is $2 (£1.30) per month.

Summary of Monthly Costs:

Cost Type	One Rabbit	Two Rabbits
Food	$30 (£19.50)	$60 (£39)
Bedding	$50 (£32.50)	$50 (£32.50)
Veterinary Care	$5 (£3.25)	$10 (£6.50)
Additional Costs	$2 (£1.30)	$4 (£2.60)
Total:	$87 (£56.55)	$124 (£80.60)

c.) Time Considerations

In addition to the initial and monthly costs for keeping Lionhead rabbits, you also need to think about the amount of care these animals require and the time that this will take. Though Lionhead rabbits are not difficult to keep as pets, they do require regular maintenance. Refer to the following lists to get an idea how much time you will need to dedicate to your rabbit's care on a daily and weekly basis:

Daily Tasks to Complete:

- Clean food dish and refresh food
- Clean water bottle and refresh water
- Moving rabbit to exercise pen (20 to 30 minutes daily)
- Interacting with the rabbit
- Observation/basic health check

Estimated Daily Commitment: 1 hour

Weekly Tasks to Complete:

- Completely replacing bedding
- Cleaning out cage and accessories
- More detailed health check
- Spending extended time interacting with rabbit
- Checking ears, nails and teeth
- Combing/brushing rabbit (when molting you may need to do this daily)

Estimated Weekly Commitment: 10 hours

5.) Human Health Considerations

Before you buy you also need to consider any implications to your own health. For example, do you know if you have an allergy or sensitivity to rabbits? I would recommendation taking advice from your Doctor to ensure that you understand that implications to your own health and if necessary, are allergy tested.

6.) Pros and Cons of Lionhead Rabbits

Before you purchase a Lionhead Rabbit you should take the time to learn the pros and cons of the breed. Different rabbit breeds require different levels of care and, if you are unprepared, you may have difficulty with your rabbits.

Below you will find a list of both the pros and cons of keeping Lionhead Rabbits to help you make an educated decision:

Pros for Lionhead Rabbits

- Remains small so they do not require very large cages
- Very friendly and social breed, make excellent pets
- Generally takes well to handling by humans
- Very attractive pets; come in all colors and patterns
- Fairly easy to care for and can be kept with certain other household pets
- An excellent choice as a pet for children

Cons for Lionhead Rabbits

- Have long, thick fur that requires more grooming than some other breeds
- You may need to avoid certain types of litter (shavings) that can get stuck in the rabbit's fur
- Double-maned rabbits may need to be trimmed occasionally to prevent matting
- May be more prone to dental problems than other breeds
- Can be difficult to treat for fleas and mites due to excess fur
- Have very sensitive digestive systems and may be more prone to intestinal problems than other breeds

Chapter Four: Purchasing Lionhead Rabbits

Once you have decided that a Lionhead Rabbit is the right pet for you, you can begin thinking about where you are going to get it. There are several options to choose from in purchasing pet rabbits and each option has its own pros and cons.

1.) Where to Buy Lionhead Rabbits

On the following pages you will find detailed information regarding purchasing Lionhead Rabbits in the U.S.A. and in the U.K.

a.) Buying in the U.S.A.

In the United States, you can purchase Lionhead Rabbits from local pet stores, licensed breeders or rabbit rescues. If you are not concerned with buying a rabbit with a certain pedigree, the easiest option may be to check out your local pet store. The availability of Lionhead Rabbits may vary by location so you may want to ask around to determine which stores will have the breed in stock and when.

Another option is to purchase your Lionhead Rabbits directly from a licensed breeder. This option will ensure that the rabbits have been properly bred and they are also more likely to have undergone genetic testing for hereditary diseases. If you plan to breed your rabbits for sale or show, it is often a better idea to buy from a licensed breeder than from a pet store.

The final option is to adopt your rabbit from a rabbit rescue or from your local humane society. These organizations do not always have baby rabbits available but you should be able to leave your contact information to receive a call if any come in.

There are benefits associated with adopting adult rabbits, however. For example, they are more likely to be litter trained already and they may have already been vaccinated and spayed/neutered. The cost of adopting a rabbit from a shelter is also likely to be a little lower than purchasing from a licensed breeder.

b.) Buying in the U.K.

Many of the same options for buying a Lionhead Rabbit in the U.S. can be found in the U.K. as well. You can, for example, find these rabbits for sale at local pet stores. Again, the availability of this particular breed may vary so it is best to contact several stores in your area to inquire about Lionhead Rabbits.

You can also purchase rabbits directly from a breeder. Keep in mind that breeders in the U.K. are not required to be licensed – it is recommended, however, that they be registered with the British Rabbit Council (BRC). You should be aware, however, that just because a breeder is recognized by the BRC doesn't mean that the rabbits are pedigree or of good show quality. Take the time to contact the breeder and view some of the rabbits before buying.

Another option is to adopt a rabbit from a local rabbit shelter or humane society. As is true in the U.S., breed availability may vary by location so it is wise to contact the shelter to ask about Lionhead Rabbits. If you are not in a hurry, you can always leave your name and number and ask to be called if a Lionhead Rabbit comes in.

****Note**: Purchasing animals online is dangerous and can be considered cruel because it is difficult to regulate the treatment of animals during shipping – they may be exposed to extreme temperatures and/or rough handling. Please avoid buying Lionhead Rabbits online. If this is your only option, then please reconsider having a pet at all. It just isn't worth it!

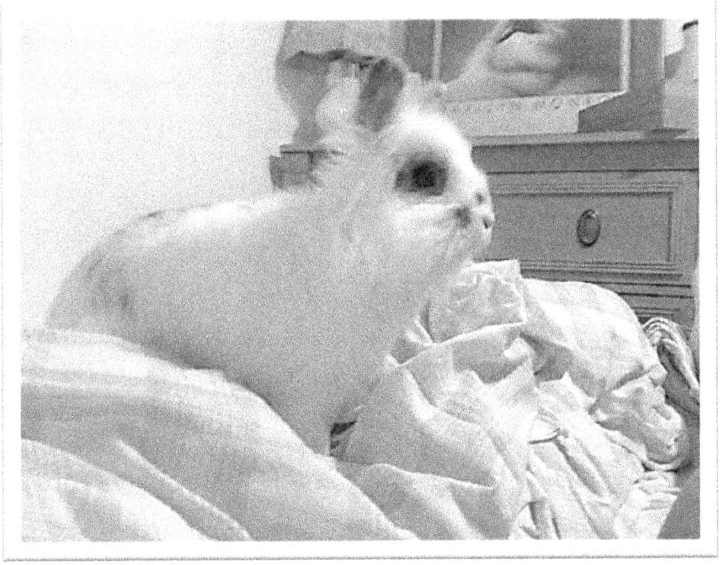

2.) How to Select a Healthy Lionhead Rabbit

One of the worst mistakes you can make as a new rabbit owner is to fall in love with a rabbit before making sure that it is healthy. Your first priority in buying a Lionhead Rabbit should be to ensure that it is in good health – this will save you a lot of money and heartache down the line.

While purchasing from a reputable breeder is a good start, you should also take the time to examine the litter before deciding which rabbit you want.

Examine the kits individually and ask yourself the following questions:

Does the rabbit appear active and curious?

- A healthy, well-socialized rabbit should not be huddled in the corner, avoiding human contact.

Are the rabbit's eyes clear, bright and free of discharge?

- If the rabbit's eyes are not clear or if they show signs of discharge, the rabbit could have an eye infection.

Are the rabbit's ears and nose clean and free of odor or discharge?

- Again, odor or discharge may be indication of an infection.

Are the rabbit's teeth properly aligned?

- In Lionhead Rabbits, a correct bite will show the top teeth just in front of and covering the bottom teeth. Improper bite can lead to serious problems down the line.

Does the rabbit's coat look healthy?

- Check for bald patches and signs of matting – you should also part the fur and check for mites or fleas.

Are the feet and nails in good condition?

- Check the bottom of the rabbit's feet to make sure there aren't any open sores. You should also check to make sure the nails are healthy and not ingrown or overgrown.

Are there signs of diarrhea?

- Carefully flip the rabbit over on its back and check the bottom – you should not see signs of wetness or feces matted in the fur. You may also want to check the cage for signs of diarrhea because this could be an indication of infection or other serious disease.

Once you have addressed all of these questions and determined that the rabbits in the litter are healthy you can move on to selecting the individual rabbit you want. If you are picking a rabbit for a pet then you can let your preferences for mane, color and pattern guide your decision.

If you intend to breed the rabbits, however, you may want to make the decision a little more carefully based on the desired results of your breeding. It may be a sound investment to ask your vet to check your new rabbit before falling in love with it and committing to buying!

Chapter Five: Caring for Lionhead Rabbits

In order to keep your Lionhead Rabbits happy and healthy you must provide them with a habitat that meets certain requirements.

The most important requirement is, of course, space. If your rabbit doesn't have adequate room to hop around, it could cause spinal problems and may also lead to obesity.

1.) Habitat Requirements

At a minimum, your rabbit's cage should be four times your rabbit's length. It should also be wide enough that your rabbit can stretch out completely without touching the sides. Lionhead Rabbits do not necessarily need very tall cages, but they cage should be tall enough that the rabbit can stand on its back legs without hitting its head on the roof of the cage.

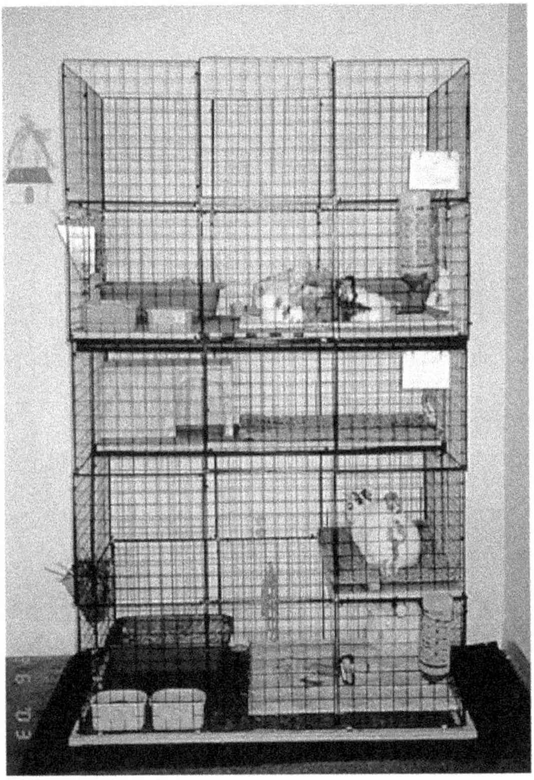

The main components of an indoor Lionhead Rabbit cage include a plastic or metal base and a wire or mesh housing. You can also find multi-level rabbit cages which are often referred to as rabbit "condos". Inside the cage you will need to provide a litter tray where your rabbit can relieve himself.

On the outside of the cage you will be able to hang a water bottle, food dish and a compartment to hold fresh hay. The organization of your rabbit cage will depend on the model and you can customize it as you like. A general rule of thumb is that bigger is better and you should get advice from a good local pet store.

a.) Types of Enclosures

If you plan to purchase an enclosure or cage for your Lionhead Rabbit you have a number of options to choose from. First you must decide whether you want to keep your rabbits indoors or outdoors, then you must choose the appropriate enclosure.

In order to make this decision, you should familiarize yourself with the pros and cons of keeping rabbits indoors vs. outdoors.

Pros of Keeping Rabbits Indoors

- Receive more attention from family members
- Protected from predators
- Less likely to contract disease (no contact with wildlife, not exposed to the elements)
- More likely to notice symptoms of disease early on
- Temperature is stable and comfortable
- Frequent interaction with human caretakers, forms a close bond with them

Cons of Keeping Rabbits Indoors

- May produce an unpleasant odor if their cage isn't cleaned often enough
- Rabbits may make noise in their cage
- Free-roaming indoor rabbits may chew on electrical wires, cords and other items
- May not get along with other household pets
- Cage takes up space – not ideal for small homes

Pros of Keeping Rabbits Outdoors

- Easier to provide a large cage

- May not need to worry about litter training
- Do not have to worry about rabbits producing odor or noise in the home although you still have to clean their cages regularly
- Rabbits have the freedom to roam where they please (in outdoor enclosures, not hutches)
- May supplement their diet by eating grass and other plants in the yard (if free roaming) although this can be a con as well if the plants are toxic or if you use pesticides which can be harmful to your rabbit

Cons of Keeping Rabbits Outdoors

- Likely to receive less attention than indoor rabbits
- If not kept with other rabbits, can become very lonely
- May be exposed to disease and parasites
- Potential danger from outdoor predators
- More stressful life, may lead to a shortened lifespan
- May not be socialized as well, might be difficult to handle
- Might be less affectionate with human caretakers

Once you've made the decision regarding whether you want to keep your Lionhead Rabbits indoors or outdoors you can move on to thinking about the specific type of cage you want to use. The type of cage you choose is very important because it will have an effect on your rabbit's health and mobility.

Types of Indoor Cages

Single-Level Cage: A single-level cage is one of the simplest options in indoor rabbit housing. These cages typically consist of a plastic or metal base and a wire frame. The benefit of these cages is that they are fairly easy to clean and they come in various sizes to accommodate a single rabbit or a pair of rabbits.

The key to choosing a single-level cage is to make sure you get one that gives your rabbit enough space. The cage should be long enough that your rabbit can make three hops from one end to the other and it should be wide enough that your rabbit can lie down across the cage. Height is less important than length, but the cage should be at least as tall as your rabbit when it stands on its hind legs.

Rabbit Condo (Multi-Level Cage): One of the most popular housing options for indoor rabbits is the rabbit condo. Rabbit condos are multi-level cages that provide space for multiple rabbits on several levels. Ramps or shelves may be installed to connect the various levels and customizations are easy.

One of the main benefits of this type of cage is that you can easily build one yourself. Using stackable wire cubes or metal fencing panels, you can build a custom condo for your Lionhead Rabbits. Be sure to include a litter pan, space for your rabbit to lie down and enough room that your rabbit can move about easily.

Pen: Another simple option in indoor rabbit housing is to construct a pen. A pen is not a traditional cage because it doesn't have a base or a roof – it simply consists of wire mesh panels attached in a circle, square or rectangle. This option will give your rabbit plenty of room to exercise and play while also providing enough space for the essentials.

One of the main benefits of a rabbit pen is that you can easily customize them to suit your needs. You can create a single, large pen for multiple rabbits or divide the pen into sections to house your rabbits separately. You can prevent your rabbits from damaging the floor by lining the pen with a toxin free plastic or by using a piece of old scrap carpeting underneath.

Free-Roaming: If you are able to successfully litter train your rabbit, you also have the option of simply letting it roam freely throughout the house. As long as you provide your rabbit with a litter pan or two, it should be fine. Though this option is the best way to give your rabbit the space it needs to exercise, it does come with potential dangers and problems.

If your rabbit isn't properly litter trained, for example, it could make a mess of your house. There is also the danger that your rabbit might chew on electric cords and hurt itself. If you choose this option for your rabbit, be sure to "rabbit-proof" your home first, making it safe for your rabbit to roam freely.

Types of Outdoor Cages

Hutch: A rabbit hutch is traditionally a wooden box with a wire mesh front. Hutches also provide an enclosed area where the rabbit can sleep and seek shelter from the elements. Like any rabbit cage, a hutch should be large enough for your rabbit to stretch out and to make several hops before reaching the other end.

If you plan to keep multiple rabbits together, you will need to use a larger hutch to accommodate them. The ASPCA recommends hutch dimensions no smaller than 4 feet x 2 feet x 2 feet (1.22 x 0.61 x 0.61 meters). In addition to the hutch itself, you will also need to provide your rabbits with several hours of exercise in a rabbit run on a daily basis.

Rabbit Shed: A rabbit shed is simply a garden shed or some other kind of small building which has been converted into a dwelling for rabbits. This type of enclosure has many benefits of other outdoor cages. For example, a shed is much larger than a rabbit hutch and it allows the rabbits to roam freely.

You can build shelves and nest boxes into the walls of the shed to provide your rabbits with exercise and recreation. Another benefit is that you can walk right into the shed to spend quality time with your Lionhead Rabbits. A shed will also keep your rabbits protected from rain and you can install a heating system to maintain a stable temperature even in the winter.

Rabbit Run: A rabbit run is an excellent way to give your outdoor rabbits a safe secure environment to allow them play time outside the hutch. The minimum size for a rabbit run should be 6 feet x 4 feet x 2 feet (1.83 x 1.22 x 0.61 meters), though larger runs are always better. A simple rabbit run might consist of a wooden frame and mesh sides and roof – this will keep your rabbit contained and safe from predators. Another option is an apex run – a triangular-shaped run made from wood, wire and mesh.

As an alternative to buying a rabbit run, you can construct one yourself using various materials. A pen made from wire panels (commonly called a puppy pen) is an easy and inexpensive option. Another option is to build one out of wood and wire mesh. Whether you buy or build a rabbit run, be sure to provide your rabbits with access to water and ensure a portion of the run provides shade on warm sunny days with shelter for wet and windy days.

Depending on where you live, please take into account the temperature to ensure that it is appropriate and comfortable for your pet. If you are using a wire or mesh run, be sure to keep an eye on your rabbits so they don't dig under it and escape!

Summary of Cage Options:

Indoor Cages

- Single-Level Cage
- Rabbit Condo (Multi-level Cage)
- Rabbit Pen
- Free-Roaming

Outdoor Cages

- Rabbit Hutch
- Rabbit Shed
- Rabbit Run

b.) Cage Accessories

In addition to the cage itself, you will also need to provide your rabbit with a few accessories. These include bowls to hold commercial pellets and fresh vegetables, a water bottle and perhaps a compartment that attaches to the side of the cage to hold fresh hay. Your rabbit may also appreciate the inclusion of hiding places and toys.

Toys for Lionhead Rabbits:

In order to keep your rabbits active, you should provide them with a selection of toys in their cage. Some of the most popular rabbit toys include:

- Wooden boxes
- Cardboard tubes
- Plastic balls
- Wooden toys for chewing
- Rabbit chew blocks

Providing your rabbit with boxes, tunnels and toys is an easy way to encourage both mental and physical stimulation. Including some wooden toys and rabbit chew blocks will help to keep your rabbit's teeth filed down. It is a good idea to keep many rabbit toys on hand, rotating them every few days to keep your rabbits from getting bored. Please ensure that toys are BPA free and non-toxic.

c.) Litter Training a Rabbit

In many cases, rabbits will litter train themselves because they are naturally clean animals. If you do need to litter train your rabbit, however, it is not difficult to do. You will need to start by isolating your rabbit in a small area without carpeting (this will make it easier to clean up any mess).

Next, prepare a litter box that is large enough for your rabbit to lie down in. Fill the litter box with about 1 inch (2.54 cm.) of non-toxic litter and cover it with a layer of hay. If you can, take some of the soiled hay from your rabbit's cage and add it to the litter box to encourage your rabbit to use it. Confine your rabbit to the area with the litter box until he begins to urinate exclusively in the litter box.

Another option is to place multiple litter boxes in your rabbit's cage. Keep an eye on your rabbit and take note of which areas he tends to choose to do his business. Keep the litter boxes in those areas and remove the rest. Your rabbit might have a few accidents outside the litter box now and then but this is normal behavior.

****Note:** Check before purchase as certain types of litter are harmful to Lionhead Rabbits including clay litter, clumping litter, pine or cedar shavings and corn cob litter.

2.) Feeding Lionhead Rabbits

Lionhead Rabbits are herbivores which means that they receive all of their daily nutrition from plant-based foods. This doesn't mean that you can give your rabbits a few carrots or a handful of lettuce every day and expect it to meet their nutritional needs. Like any other animal, these rabbits require a balanced diet including carbohydrates, lipids and protein. The best way to achieve this for your rabbits is to offer them a varied diet.

a.) How Much to Feed

The amount you need to feed your Lionhead Rabbits depends on their size and age. Both juvenile and adult rabbits should have free access to unlimited amounts of dried grass or hay. Adult rabbits should also be given some kind of fresh vegetable but these should be introduced into their diet slowly after the rabbit reaches 1 year of age. Adding too much fiber to the diet at once can cause digestive issues because Lionhead Rabbits have sensitive stomachs.

In addition to hay, grass and vegetables you should also give your rabbits some commercial rabbit pellets on a daily basis. For adult rabbits, about 2.5 oz. (70.9 g.) should be sufficient. Baby rabbits, on the other hand, should be given between 2.5 and 3 oz. (70.9 to 85 g.) because they need the extra nutrition to grow properly. In the following sections you will learn more about what types of foods to offer your rabbits.

b.) Nutritional Needs of Rabbits

Lionhead Rabbits have very high metabolic rates so it is essential to feed them the right foods so their nutritional needs will be met. Fiber is one of the most important aspects of a rabbit's diet – it helps promote healthy digestion and also helps to absorb bacterial toxins.

The following table describes the nutritional requirements of Lionhead Rabbits. The numbers listed indicate percentage each nutrient should compose of the rabbit's daily diet.

Life Stage	% Protein	% Fat	% Fiber	% Carbohydrate
Juvenile	16	2-4	14-16	45-50
Adult	12	1.5-2	14-16	40-45
Pregnant	15	2-3	14-16	45-50
Lactating	17	2.5-3.5	12-14	45-50

In addition to these nutrients, rabbits also require unlimited access to fresh water. It is also important to note that any changes you make to your rabbit's diet should be done gradually. Because Lionhead Rabbits have such sensitive digestive systems, any sudden or drastic change in their diet could cause health problems.

c.) Commercial Pellets

Part of your rabbit's diet should be made up of high-quality commercial rabbit pellets. These foods help to balance out your rabbit's nutrition, filling in the gaps left by hay, grasses and vegetables. It is important to buy a high-quality pellet for your rabbits because low-quality pellets are likely to contain fillers and other ingredients that do not add to the nutritional content of the product.

Though it is a good idea to offer your rabbits some commercial food on a daily basis, it should not compose the majority of their diet. Overfeeding with commercial foods can lead to kidney damage and other health problems. You should also avoid using commercial food that has been sitting on the shelf for too long. Commercial pellets can only be considered "fresh" for about one month so do not try to buy your rabbit food in bulk if you will not be able to use it up within one month.

d.) Other Food

In addition to commercial pellets, Lionhead Rabbits enjoy hay, grain, grass and fresh vegetables. You can buy hay and grass in a variety of different forms – it may be fresh, freeze-dried or formed into cubes. You may want to try out a few different kinds to see what your rabbit likes best.

The best types of grass hay for Lionhead Rabbits are Timothy and meadow hay. These hays have high levels of fiber. Alfalfa and clover hays are high in protein and calcium which is good for your rabbits in small quantities but too much can result in kidney damage. Legume hays like alfalfa and clover are, however, suitable for juvenile and pregnant or nursing rabbits.

Water is another essential element of a Lionhead Rabbit's diet. Your rabbits should have constant access to fresh water through sipper bottles – water bowls are not recommended because they can easily be contaminated by food, bedding, feces and urine. If you keep your rabbits outdoors, you may need to take precautions against the water bottle freezing. Anti-freezing agents like Vyderphor can be used to treat water bottles so they do not freeze in the winter or turn green in the summer.

Vegetables are another important aspect of a rabbit's daily diet. It is important, however, that you introduce vegetables into your rabbit's diet slowly so as not to cause digestive upset. When possible, offer your rabbits organic vegetables to avoid exposing them to harmful pesticides and herbicides. Even if the vegetables are organic, you should still be sure to wash them before giving them to your rabbit.

Some of the best vegetables to give rabbits include lettuces and other leafy greens, broccoli, fresh herbs, celery, watercress and carrot or radish tops.

Avoid feeding your Lionhead Rabbit the following vegetables:

- Corn
- Iceberg Lettuce
- Peas
- Pennyroyal Mint
- Potatoes

****Note:** You should also limit the amount of spinach and celery you offer your rabbits because these foods are lower in nutritional content than other vegetables.

I would recommend that you check with your veterinarian or breeder before introducing any new foods to your rabbit that they have not previously recommended.

Food Safe for Rabbits

Apples

Beans

Blueberries

Carrots

Cherries

Dandelion Greens

Grapes

Kale

Mustard Greens

Mango

Melon

Orange

Pear

Papaya

Pineapple

Peach

Peas

Parsnip

Parsley

Raspberries

Strawberries

Tomatoes (fruit)

Plants Toxic to Rabbits

There are some plants that are considered toxic to rabbits and they include:

Acorns	Juniper
Aloe	Jack-in-the-Pulpit
Apple Seeds	Laurel Lupine
Almonds	Lily of the Valley
Asparagus Fern	Marigold
Azalea	Milkweed
Carnations	Mistletoe
Clematis	Nutmeg
Daffodil Bulbs	Oak
Eucalyptus	Parsnip
Fruit Pits	Poppy
Fruit Seeds	Peony
Geranium	Philodendron
Gladiola	Poinsettia
Hemlock	Rhubarb Leaves
Hyacinth Bulbs	Sweet Potato
Impatiens	Tansy
Iris	Tomato Leaves
Ivy	Tulip Bulbs
Jasmine	Violet
Jessamine	Yew

*This list is not comprehensive; in order to determine whether a specific plant is toxic for rabbits, consult the House Rabbit Society website: http://rabbit.org/poisonous-plants/

Chapter Six: Keeping Lionhead Rabbits Healthy

** **Note:** This section may be upsetting to any children who may read it. Sadly like all our pets, Lionhead Rabbits are susceptible to developing certain health issues.

In order to keep your Lionhead Rabbit happy and healthy, you need to keep its cage clean and offer it a varied, high-quality diet. You should familiarize yourself with some of the diseases most commonly affecting this breed.

If you know the symptoms and warning signs, you can quickly make a diagnosis and seek the proper treatment for your pet – the sooner you take action, the greater your rabbit's chances for making a full recovery.

1.) Common Health Problems

The details in this section are not exhaustive and not designed to take the place of a qualified veterinarian who will have up to date knowledge and information regarding current treatments for any ailments. It is important to remember that although some health conditions affecting Lionhead Rabbits can be treated at home, severe cases should always be examined by a veterinarian. If you are in any doubt or the disease is impacting your rabbit's health or mobility, do not delay in taking it to the vet.

Colibacillosis

Colibacillosis is characterized by severe diarrhea and it is often caused by *Escherichia coli*. This disease can be seen in two forms depending on the rabbit's age. Newborn rabbits may exhibit a yellowish diarrhea – in newborns, this condition is often fatal and can affect the entire litter. In weaned rabbits, the intestines may fill with fluid and hemorrhages may surface.

In the case of weaned rabbits, the disease is typically fatal within 2 weeks. If the rabbit survives, it is likely to be stunted. Treatment is not often successful but, in mild cases, antibiotics may help. Rabbits that are severely affected with this disease should be culled to avoid the spread of the disease.

Causes: Escherichia coli

Symptoms: yellowish diarrhea in newborns; fluid-filled intestines and hemorrhages in weaned rabbits

Treatment: antibiotics; treatment is not often effective

Dental Problems

All rabbits, including Lionhead rabbits, are prone to developing dental problems. The most common issues are overgrown molars and enamel spurs. Your rabbit's teeth may become overgrown or develop spurs if you don't provide enough fiber-rich foods. Fibrous foods are naturally abrasive which helps to keep your rabbit's teeth filed down. In most cases, dental problems require veterinary treatment.

Causes: diet too low in fiber

Symptoms: overgrown molars, enamel spurs

Treatment: veterinary exam and treatment

Dermatophytosis

Also known as ringworm, dermatophytosis caused by either *Trichophyton mentagrophytes* or *Microsporum canis*. These infections typically result from poor husbandry or inadequate nutrition. Ringworm can be transmitted through direct contact with an infected rabbit or sharing tools such as brushes. The symptoms of ringworm include circular raised bumps on the body. The skin is these areas may be red and capped with a white, flaky material. Some of the most common treatments for ring worm include topical antifungal creams that contain miconazole or itraconazole. A 1% copper sulfate dip may also be effective.

Causes: *Trichophyton mentagrophytes* or *Microsporum canis*; typically results from poor husbandry or inadequate nutrition

Symptoms: circular raised bumps on the body; skin is red and capped with a white, flaky material

Treatment: include topical antifungal creams that contain miconazole or itraconazole; 1% copper sulfate dip

Enterotoxemia

Enterotoxemia is a disease characterized by explosive diarrhea and it typically affects rabbits between the ages of 4 and 8 weeks. Symptoms of this condition include lethargy, loss of condition and greenish-brown fecal matter around the perianal area. In many cases, this condition is fatal within 48 hours.

The primary cause of this disease is *Clostridium spiroforme*. These organisms are common in rabbits in small numbers but they can become a problem when the rabbit's diet is too low in fiber. Treatment may not be effective due to the rapid progression of the disease but adding cholestryamine or copper sulfate to the diet can help prevent enterotoxemia. Reducing stress in young rabbits and increasing fiber intake can also help.

Causes: Clostridium spiroforme

Symptoms: lethargy, loss of condition and greenish-brown fecal matter around the perianal area

Treatment: may not be effective; adding cholestryamine or copper sulfate to the diet can help prevent

Fleas/Mites

Indoor rabbits are unlikely to contract fleas and ticks on their own. If your rabbit spends time outside or if you have other pets that spend time outside, however, your rabbit could be at risk. Mites are typically found in the ears and fur of rabbits and they most often present themselves after your rabbit's immune system has already been compromised.

Fur mites tend to stay at the base of the neck or near the rabbit's rear. If left untreated, mites and fleas can cause severe itching, bald spots and bleeding. The best treatment for fleas and mites is a prescription medication called Revolution, known in the UK as Stronghold. Another treatment option in the UK is Ivermectin drops.

Causes: exposure to infested pets, spending time outside

Symptoms: itching, bald spots, bleeding

Treatment: prescription medication; Revolution in the USA, known in the UK as Stronghold or Ivermectin drops.

Listeriosis

Listeriosis is a type of sporadic septicemia which often causes sudden death or abortion – this condition is most common in pregnant Does. Some of the contributing factors for this disease include poor husbandry and stress. Some of the common symptoms include anorexia, depression and weight loss.

If not properly treated, the *Listeria monocytogenes* responsible for the disease can spread to the blood, liver and uterus. Treatment is not often attempted because diagnosis is not frequently made premortem.

Causes: Listeria monocytogenes

Symptoms: anorexia, depression and weight loss; often causes sudden death or abortion

Treatment: not often attempted because diagnosis is not frequently made premortem

Mastitis

This condition is most commonly seen in rabbitries but it can affect single rabbits. Mastitis is a condition that affects pregnant Does and it is caused by *staphylococci* bacteria. The bacteria infect the mammary glands, causing them to become hot, red and swollen. If the disease is allowed to progress, it may cause septicemia and become fatal.

Does affected by mastitis are unlikely to eat but they will crave water. The rabbit may also run a fever. Treatment for this condition may include antibiotic treatment. Penicillin, however, should be avoided because it can cause diarrhea. Kits should not be fostered because they will only end up spreading the disease.

Causes: *staphylococci* bacteria

Symptoms: hot, red and swollen mammary glands; loss of appetite; fever

Treatment: antibiotics

Myxomatosis

Myxomatosis is a viral disease that is caused by *myxoma* virus. This condition is typically fatal and it can be transmitted through direct contact or through biting insects. Some of the initial symptoms of the disease include conjunctivitis, eye discharge, listlessness, anorexia and fever. In severe cases, death may occur after only 48 hours.

Treatment for this condition is generally not effective and it can cause severe and lasting damage. A vaccine is available to be given after the rabbit reaches 6 weeks of age.

Causes: by *myxoma* virus; transmitted through direct contact or through biting insects

Symptoms: conjunctivitis, eye discharge, listlessness, anorexia and fever

Treatment: generally not effective; vaccine is available

Otitis Media

Also called "wry neck" or "head tilt," otitis media is caused by an infection resulting from *P multocida* or *Encephalitozoon cunuculi*. These bacteria cause the accumulation of fluid or pus in the ear, causing the rabbit to tilt its head. Antibiotic therapy may be effective, though it may just worsen the condition. In most cases, rabbits infected with this condition are culled.

Causes: *P multocida* or *Encephalitozoon cunuculi* bacteria

Symptoms: accumulation of fluid or pus in the ear, causing the rabbit to tilt its head

Treatment: antibiotic therapy may be effective

Papillomatosis

Papillomatosis is fairly common in domestic rabbits and it is caused by the *rabbit oral papillomavirus*. This disease results in the formation of small grey nodules or warts on the underside of the tongue or floor of the mouth. Another type, caused by *cottontail papillomavirus*, may produce horned warts on the neck, shoulders, ears and abdomen. There is no treatment for these conditions but the lesions typically go away on their own in time.

Causes: rabbit oral papillomavirus, cottontail papillomavirus

Symptoms: small grey nodules or warts on the underside of the tongue or floor of the mouth or horned warts on the neck, shoulders, ears and abdomen

Treatment: no treatment; the lesions typically go away on their own in time

Parasites

One of the most common parasites found in rabbits is *Encephalitozoon cuniculi*. This protozoan parasite can survive in the body for years without causing any harm. In some cases, however, the parasite can cause severe damage. This parasite typically causes nerve damage which results in head tilting, incontinence, paralysis and rupture of the lens of the eye.

Intestinal worms are also a common problem in rabbits. Both of these conditions can be treated with de-worming paste. This treatment can be used for infected rabbits and as a preventive against parasites. When used as a preventive, the paste is typically administered twice a year.

Causes: Encephalitozoon cuniculi, intestinal worms

Symptoms: head tilting, incontinence, paralysis and rupture of the lens of the eye

Treatment: de-worming paste

Pneumonia

Pneumonia is fairly common in domestic rabbits and it is most often a secondary infection. The most common cause of pneumonia in rabbits is *P multocida* bacteria, though other kinds may be involved. A precursor of pneumonia is often upper respiratory disease which may be a result of inadequate ventilation or sanitation.

Some of the common symptoms of pneumonia include listlessness, fever and anorexia. Once they show symptoms, most rabbits succumb to the infection within 1 week. Though antibiotic treatment is often used, it is not typically effective because it may not be administered until the disease is highly advanced.

Causes: *P multocida* bacteria

Symptoms: listlessness, fever and anorexia

Treatment: antibiotic treatment is often used but not typically effective

Rhinitis

Rhinitis is the medical term used to describe sniffling or chronic inflammation in the airway and lungs. This condition is often caused by *Pastuerella,* though *Staphylococcus* or *Streptococcus* may also be involved. The initial symptom of this disease is a thin stream of mucus flowing from the nose. As the disease progresses, the flow may encrust the fur on the paws and chest. Sneezing and coughing may also be exhibited. This condition generally resolves itself but even recovered rabbits can be carriers of the disease.

Causes: is often caused by *Pastuerella,* though *Staphylococcus* or *Streptococcus* may also be involved

Symptoms: sniffling or chronic inflammation in the airway and lungs; thin stream of mucus flowing from the nose

Treatment: generally resolves itself

Uterine Cancer

A common cause of death in female rabbits, uterine cancer can easily be prevented. Spaying female rabbits between the ages of 5 months and 2 years is the best way to prevent this disease. In un-spayed female rabbits, uterine cancer can spread to several different organs before the disease is diagnosed. At that point, treatment is typically ineffective.

Causes: tumor growing in the uterus

Symptoms: other reproductive issues; endometriosis, bulging veins, vaginal discharge, bloody urine

Treatment: spaying female rabbits to prevent; once the cancer develops, treatment is generally ineffective

Viral Hemorrhagic Disease

Also called rabbit hemorrhagic disease, viral hemorrhagic disease is caused by *rabbit calcivirus* transmitted through direct contact or contaminated food, water and bedding. Unfortunately, there is no effective treatment for this condition and many rabbits die from it without ever showing symptoms.

Some of the most common symptoms of viral hemorrhagic disease include difficulty breathing, paralysis, lethargy, bloody discharge from the nose, weight loss and convulsions. Once symptoms appear, the disease is typically fatal within 2 weeks.

Causes: *rabbit calcivirus*; transmitted through direct contact or contaminated food, water and bedding

Symptoms: difficulty breathing, paralysis, lethargy, bloody discharge from the nose, weight loss and convulsions

Treatment: no effective treatment

Wool Block

All breeds are prone to developing a dangerous condition called Wool Block although it is most prevalent in wooly breeds. Wool Block occurs when a ball of hair forms in the stomach and intestines of the rabbit, preventing it from digesting any food. This can lead to inadequate nutrition and eventual starvation and death.

Rabbits are incapable of vomiting to clear the hairball. It is recommended that you speak to your breeder before purchasing your rabbit as some people feel that a pre-disposition to wool block can be inherited. You can check with your breeder whether it is a problem that they have experienced with their stock.

There are several things that you can do to help prevent and diagnose wool block. Your rabbit must have access to fresh de-chlorinated water at all times and should have lots of exercise. It is essential that your rabbit is fed with a diet that is high in fiber and contains plenty of hay.

Many owners supplement with papaya tablets or fresh papaya or pineapple chunks once a week as the enzymes in these help dissolve the food within the fiber and therefore allow it to be passed more easily through the intestines. Other owners will on one day each week feed their rabbit hay and two tablespoons of whole oats and/or extra fresh vegetables. On this day, they do not feed their rabbit any pellets, allowing their stomach an opportunity to clean out. You should also ensure that your rabbit is groomed properly to reduce the amount of hair that they ingest.

Additionally you should study their droppings each day and become familiar with what is normal for your rabbit and note any changes. Droppings that become smaller or are a string of beads mixed with hair, can be a sign of wool block. Due to the seriousness of this condition, if you are in any doubt, you should seek veterinarian advice immediately.

Causes: Ball of hair in the stomach and intestines

Symptoms: Changes in eating patterns, weight loss, change in droppings, lethargy

Treatment: Seek veterinarian attention as opinions vary on treatment

2.) Preventing Illness

There are several things you can do to help protect your rabbit against disease. The most important thing is to provide your rabbit with a clean, healthy environment. It is essential that you clean your rabbit's cage on a regular basis and provide plenty of fresh de-chlorinated water for him to drink. You should also be sure to provide a healthy, varied diet that meets all of your rabbit's nutritional needs.

a.) Dangerous/Toxic Foods

There are certain foods and plants which can be very harmful for your Lionhead Rabbit. Please refer to the list of foods that can cause serious problems in the Feeding Lionhead Rabbits section in Chapter Five. You can also check with your vet or local breeder on any local foodstuffs that you might consider feeding your rabbit to avoid heartache.

b.) Recommended Vaccinations

Having your rabbit vaccinated is one of the best things you can do to protect it from disease. Two of the most important vaccines for Lionhead Rabbits are against myxomatosis and viral hemorrhagic disease (VHD) – both of these vaccinations are highly recommended.

These vaccines are available as single vaccines, which need to be taken nine days apart every six months, or as a single combined vaccine once a year. The recommended vaccines for your rabbit will depend on where you live and your vet can advise you what is required.

It is a good idea to have your rabbit examined as soon as possible by a vet after you bring it home. Your vet will be able to assess your rabbit's condition and set a schedule for future check-ups. Additionally, your vet will also offer recommendations on what vaccines your pet needs and how often he needs them. This will vary from area to area so getting up to date local knowledge is essential.

It may seem like a needless cost to take your rabbit to the vet once a year but it can save you a lot of money and heartache in diagnosing serious diseases before they become untreatable.

c.) Ears, Eyes, Nails and Teeth

In addition to vaccinating your rabbit you should also check its condition on your own from time to time. Take a look inside your rabbit's ears for signs of wax buildup or infection – unpleasant odor may also be a sign of infection. Your rabbit's feet should be dry and free from sores. If you notice patches of skin where the fur has worn away or swelling, you should seek immediate veterinary care.

When petting your rabbit, take the time to check its skin and coat. If you notice white flakes or tiny white dots, your rabbit could have mites or fleas.

A rabbit's nails grow continuously so you will need to trim them every six to eight weeks. Trimming your rabbit's nails is not a difficult task but it does require a degree of caution. Inside your rabbit's nail lies the quick – a vein which supplies blood to the nail. If you cut your rabbit's nails too short, you could sever the quick and induce severe bleeding. When clipping your rabbit's nails it is best to only cut off the pointed tip. To be safe, have your veterinarian show you how to properly trim a rabbit's nails before you try it yourself.

One of the most common causes of runny eyes in rabbits is a bacterial eye infection. These infections can be very dangerous and must be treated by a veterinarian as soon as possible. In many cases, antibiotics will be prescribed to handle the infection.

Obstructions and inflammation in the eye may be the result of natural or unnatural causes. In some cases, a piece of bedding or some other object may get stuck in the eye causing it to water or become inflamed. It is also possible, however, for a misshapen eyelid or part of the bone in the rabbit's face to cause an obstruction. If the flow of tears is obstructed, they may form a path down the cheek, discoloring the fur. Depending on the cause of the obstruction, surgery may be necessary to correct the issue.

If the rabbit's eyes do not produce enough tears on their own, they may become dry and irritated. When the eyes become too dry, they are more prone to scratches and erosions which can have a devastating effect on your rabbit's ability to see properly. Some of the symptoms of dry eyes include squinting, eye discharge, redness and inflammation. Trauma to the eye can also interfere with the production of tears and should be evaluated by a veterinarian.

Depending what type of litter you use in your rabbit's cage, your rabbit could develop watery eyes as a result of allergies. Dust from the litter, hay or food in your rabbit's cage can get into the eyes and cause irritation. To prevent this from happening, choose litter that is dust-free and make sure the cage is well ventilated.

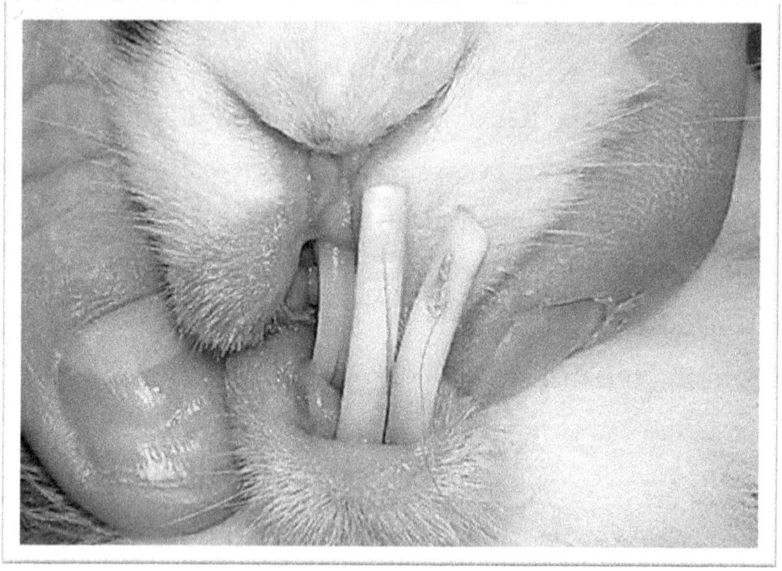

In some rabbits, the teeth are not properly aligned, a condition called malocclusion.

If your rabbit's teeth are not properly aligned they can develop a condition called malocclusion. There are three main causes of this, the most common being genetic predisposition, injury or bacterial infection. If you provide your rabbit with adequate chew toys, you shouldn't have to worry about its teeth becoming overgrown.

You should, however, make frequent checks to see if the teeth are properly aligned – if they aren't, your rabbit could develop molar spurs or abscesses in the mouth.

3) Pet Insurance

Many pet owners have discovered that pet insurance helps defray the costs of veterinary expenses. Pet insurance is similar to health insurance in that you pay a monthly premium and a deductible (excess in the UK) and the pet insurance pays for whatever is covered in your plan and can include annual exams and blood work. Shopping for pet insurance is similar to shopping for health insurance in the United States. As with health insurance, the age and the overall health of your rabbit will determine how much you will pay in premiums and deductibles.

Ask plenty of questions to determine the best company and plan for your needs. Some of the questions that you should ask are:

- Can you go to your regular vet, or do you have to go to a vet assigned by the pet insurance company?
- What does the insurance plan cover? Does it cover annual exams? Surgeries? Emergency illness and injury?
- Does coverage begin immediately?
- Are pre-existing conditions covered? In addition, if your rabbit develops a health issue and you later have to renew the policy,

is that condition covered when you renew your policy?

- Is medication covered?
- Do you have to have pre-authorization before your pet receives treatment? What happens if your rabbit has the treatment without pre-authorization?
- Is there a lifetime maximum benefit amount? If so, how much is that amount?

Take the time to research your pet insurance options. Compare the different plans available, what each covers, and the cost before making the decision on which is best for you and your pet. Of course, pet insurance may not be the answer for everyone.

While pet insurance may not be a feasible option for you, consider having a backup plan, just in case your rabbit requires emergency care or you run into unexpected veterinarian costs.

A simple way to prepare for an emergency is to start a veterinary fund for your rabbit. Decide to put a certain amount of money aside each week, each month, or each paycheck to use in the case of an emergency. Think about the potential financial costs of veterinary care and plan for how you will pay for it now instead of waiting until something occurs.

4.) Planning for the Unexpected

If something happens to you, you want to know that your rabbit and any other pets will be properly cared for and loved. Some cell phones allow you to input an ICE (In Case of Emergency) number with notes. If your cell phone has such an option, use it. If it does not, write the following information on a piece of a paper and put it in your wallet with your driver's license:

- The names of each of your pets, including your rabbit.
- The names and phone numbers of family members or friends who have agreed to temporarily care for your pets in an emergency.
- The name and phone number of your veterinarian.

Be sure to also talk with your neighbors, letting them know how many pets you have and the type of pets. That way, if something happens to you, they can alert the authorities, ensuring your pets do not linger for days before they are found.

If you fail to do that and something happens to you, someone will find your rabbit and any other pets and will need to know what to do to ensure that they are cared for. It is a good idea in the case of an emergency, to ask several friends or family members to be responsible for taking care of your pets should something happen to you.

Prepare instructions for the intended guardians, providing amended instructions as necessary. Also, be sure to provide each individual with a key to your home (remember to inform your home insurance company so that this does not affect your coverage). Instructions should include:

- The name and phone numbers of each individual who agreed to take care of your rabbit and other pets.
- Your pet's diet and feeding schedule.
- The name and phone number of your veterinarian.
- Any health problems and medications your rabbit may take on a daily basis, including dosage instructions, instructions on how to give the medicine, and where the medicine is kept.

Put as much information as necessary to ensure the guardians can provide the same level of care to which your rabbit is accustomed.

Chapter Seven: Breeding Lionhead Rabbits

Like all rabbit varieties, Lionhead Rabbits are eager breeders – they can produce dozens of babies each year under the right conditions. If you want to ensure the health and wellness of your rabbits, however, you should take a few precautions in breeding them.

In order to breed your rabbits properly you should take the time to select the right breeding pair, ensure that the rabbits themselves are healthy enough for breeding and make the necessary preparations to care for the young.

a.) Basic Breeding Information

You may already be aware that a female rabbit is called a Doe and a male rabbit is called a Buck. In regards to breeding, a mother rabbit is referred to as a Dam and the father a Sire.

After a pair of rabbits has been mated, and if the female becomes pregnant, she will enter what is called a gestation period – this is the period during which the young develop inside the mother's body. This period typically lasts about 31 days and, at the end, a group of babies called kits will be born. A group of rabbit babies is collectively referred to as a litter.

The Lionhead Rabbit Doe typically reaches sexual maturity around 5 months of age – Bucks may need an extra month to mature. The term sexual maturity simply means that the rabbit is old enough to breed. Before you breed your rabbits, it is wise to take a few precautions.

First, you should never breed rabbits of two different breeds – you should also avoid breeding rabbits from the same litter because this will result in inbreeding. It is also a good idea to examine the rabbits you intend to breed to ensure that they are in good health for breeding.

****Note:** If you are keeping multiple Lionhead Rabbits together, be sure not to keep males and females in the same cage past 3 months of age. Not only will this prevent unwanted breeding but it will also allow your rabbits to mature faster.

b.) The Breeding Process

Rabbit Does of all breeds go through the estrus cycle, or "heat," so often that the cycle is generally considered to be almost continuous. This means that a female rabbit can become pregnant again almost immediately after giving birth. The number of eggs available for fertilization, however, decreases with age. Rabbits are most fertile between the ages of 6 months and 3 years. The average Lionhead Rabbit Doe can carry between 1 and 8 fertilized eggs, though 4 is the average.

In order to breed your rabbits, it is best to select the pair you intend to breed ahead of time. If you are going for a certain color, pattern or mane type you will need to be selective in your breeding choices. Once you've selected the right pair and have determined that they are healthy enough for breeding you can then introduce the female rabbit into the male rabbit's cage.

It is better to put the female in the male rabbit's cage rather than the other way around because this will increase the likelihood of mating – if you introduce the male to the female's cage he may be distracted by exploring and smelling the cage and will be less likely to mate.

It is up to you how long you choose to leave the Doe in the cage with the Buck. Some breeders observe the rabbits and remove the Doe as soon as breeding has occurred while others leave the Doe in overnight. Either way, you should avoid keeping the Doe in with the Buck for longer than 12 hours.

Once pregnancy has occurred, the Doe will enter the gestation period. This is the period during which the fertilized eggs develop inside the mother's body and it typically lasts about 31 days. You should always keep track of the dates on which you breed your rabbits. This will help you to keep track of the age of your rabbits and will also ensure that you achieve the proper timing in providing a nest box for your pregnant Does.

When female Lionhead Rabbits approach their due date, they will begin to pull fur off their bodies to form a nest for their young. It is recommended that you provide a nest box measuring about 12 inches (30.5 cm.) long by 8 inches (20.3 cm.) tall and wide for your rabbit to give birth in. You should install the box on the 28th day after conception – if you put it in any sooner, your rabbit may use the box, defecating in it and making it an unsuitable environment for newborn young.

Female Lionhead Rabbits typically give birth at night and it doesn't take more than 10 minutes for her to deliver the entire litter. After the litter has been born, the mother rabbit will cover them with fur and leave the nesting box. It may be as long as two days before the Dam begins feeding her babies, but this is not unusual.

You should never touch or move the babies but you may want to check on them every few days to make sure they are eating. Baby rabbits are born with very little hair and with closed eyes – the eyes will begin to open on the 10th day after birth at which point you should check them for eye infections.

c.) Raising Baby Rabbits

Baby Lionhead Rabbits will begin to develop fur as they age and they will begin to eat solid food after about 10 days. As long as the temperature is warm enough (above 60°F/15.6°C) you can remove the nest box from the cage after two weeks. After four weeks, you should begin weaning the kits off their mother's milk. Some mothers will naturally wean their babies so you may not need to do anything at all. If the kits are still nursing at 6 weeks of age, however, you should separate them from the mother.

Some breeders recommend keeping one baby with the mother after weaning the others. It will take time for the

Dam's breasts to get used to not nursing and leaving one baby with her will reduce the pain of weaning. You can leave the single kit with the mother for another week after removing the others before weaning it as well. After weaning, you can keep the kits together until they are 3 months old – at this point, it is best to separate the sexes to prevent unwanted breeding.

Breeding Tips

Sexual Maturity: Does at 5 months, Bucks at 6 months

Estrus Cycle: almost continuous

Kits per Litter: up to 8

Preparation for Breeding: set up a nesting box on the 28th day after conception

Gestation: 31 days, give or take 2 days

Weaning: as early as 4 weeks after birth (up to 6 weeks)

Chapter Eight: Showing Lionhead Rabbits

Showing your Lionhead Rabbit can be a fun adventure and a challenge. Lionheads are a recognized breed by the British Rabbit Council (BRC) and officially recognized as a breed with the American Rabbit Breeders Association (ARBA) as of February 1, 2014. They are now eligible to be shown and compete for Best in Show and Grand Champion status.

British Rabbit Council (BRC) standard summary:

- Adult rabbits should weigh around 3.5 lbs. (1.59 kg.) but no more than 3.75 lbs. (1.70 kg.)
- The rabbit's ears should not be more than 2.95 inches (7.5 cm) long
- The mane should be between 1.97 to 2.76 inches (5 to 7 cm.) in length
- If present, the skirt should not be longer than 2 inches (5.08 cm.)
- Other disqualifications include incorrect bite and mismatched toenails

Full details of the breed standard can be seen at the British Rabbit Council (BRC) website at the following link: www.thebrc.org/standards/F11-Lionhead.pdf

A breakdown of the standard of points is as follows:

Type = 25 points

Mane/Chest = 30 points

Coat = 25 points

Color = 10 points

Condition = 10 points

Total = 100 points

Once the show begins, you will be required to position your Lionhead Rabbit on the judging table. The rabbit should be posed so as to display its full chest and mane. Judges will evaluate your rabbit on its adherence to the breed standard and reward points accordingly.

American Rabbit Breeders Association (ARBA) standard:

Summary:

- Senior Buck and Does - 6 months of age and over, not over 3 .75 lbs. (1.70 kg.)
- Junior Bucks and Does - Under 6 months of age, not over 3.5 lbs. (1.59 kg.). Minimum weight 1.10 lbs (0.50 kg.)
- The rabbit's ears should not be more than 3.5 inches (8.89 cm) in length
- The mane must be at least 2 inches (5.08 cm) in length and form a full circle around the head which may extend into a "V" at the back of the neck
- Transition wool should not be longer than 2 inches (5.08cm).

Full details of the breed standard can be seen at the American Rabbit Breeders Association (ARBA) website at the following links: www.arba.net/standards.htm www.arba.net/PDFs/SOP_inserts.pdf

A breakdown of the standard of points is as follows:

General Type = 40

- Body = 25
- Head = 10
- Ears = 5

Fur = 45

- Mane = 35
- Coat = 10

Color = 10

Condition = 5

TOTAL = 100

Lionheads should be posed with front feet resting lightly on the judging table. When viewed from the front, the stance is high enough to show full chest and mane. In order to correctly evaluate head mount and stance, the head should not be pushed or forced down.

1.) What to Know Before Showing

The key to success in rabbit shows is to be prepared. This involves making sure your rabbit meets the breed standard and arranging the rabbit properly for judging. You should also prepare yourself by bringing along an emergency kit, just in case.

Included in your emergency kit should be:

- Nail clippers – for emergency nail trimming
- Antibiotic ointment
- Band-Aids – for minor injuries to self, not rabbit
- Hydrogen peroxide – for cleaning injuries and spots on white coats
- Slicker brush – to smooth rough coats
- Black felt-tip pen
- Business cards
- Paper towels – because you never know
- Scrap carpet square – for last-minute grooming
- Collapsible stool – when chairs are not available
- Extra clothes
- Supplies for your rabbits

2.) Tips for Finding a Show in Your Area

Finding rabbit shows in your area is not difficult if you know where to look. In most cases, you can find a list of shows on the ARBA or BRC website. The links for these sites are below:

ARBA Sanctioned Shows:
www.arba.net/showsSearch.php

The BRC Show Diary:
www.thebrc.org/shows-current-year.htm

Chapter Nine: Lionhead Rabbit Care Sheet

Basic Information:

Scientific Name: *Oryctolagus cuniculus*

Size: 2 ½ to 3 lbs. at maturity (1.13 to 1.36 kg.)

Coloration: any color or pattern is acceptable

Build: small and compact

Lifespan: 7 to 9 years

Diet: herbivorous

Foods: hay, grains, vegetables and commercial rabbit pellets

Feeding Tips: avoid feeding too many pellets or root vegetables (can result in diarrhea or dental problems)

Supplements: generally not required if the diet is sufficient in fiber and protein

<u>Cage Set-Up Guide:</u>

Minimum Size: 36 by 48 inches (91.4 by 122 cm

Material: solid floor with wire top/sides (can also be kept outdoors in a wood/wire hutch)

Decorations: toys and hiding places

Additional Items: food bowl, water bottle, bedding, grooming tools, nail trimmers, cleaning brushes

Indoor Cage Options: single-level cage, rabbit condo, rabbit pen, free-roaming

Outdoor Cage Options: hutch, rabbit shed, rabbit run

a.) Holding Your Rabbit

It is important to remember that Lionhead Rabbits are fragile creatures so you need to use caution when handling them. The first thing you need to know is that you must never pick up your rabbit by the ears. When you first bring your rabbit home you should give it a day or two to get used to the new environment before you try to hold it.

When you feel your rabbit is ready, offer it a few treats to encourage the rabbit to approach you on its own. Once your rabbit approaches you, begin petting it gently on the back and ears. If your rabbit responds well to this treatment you can try picking it up. Make sure to support your rabbit's feet and hold the rabbit's body against your chest.

b.) Introducing Your Rabbit to Children

Lionhead Rabbits are a very gentle breed so they have the capacity to get along with children. If your children are not properly educated in how to handle the rabbit, however, it could result in accidental injury. Before you bring your rabbit home, make sure to talk to your children about the responsibilities of their new pet. Teach your children how to properly hold the rabbit and warn them that the rabbit might be frightened by loud noises.

Once you bring your rabbit home, give it time to acclimate to its new surroundings. After your rabbit has become comfortable at home you can try introducing it to your kids. Hold the rabbit securely in your arms and let your child pet it gently. If your rabbit is calm, you can try setting it down on the ground so your child can pet it. Do not let your children pick the rabbit up unless they are old enough to know how to do so properly.

c.) Shedding in Rabbits

Some rabbits shed more than others but most breeds shed every three months. Because Lionhead Rabbits have long fur in their manes, they may shed a little during the time in between. Like cats, rabbits are very clean animals and they like to groom themselves. Unlike cats, however, rabbits cannot vomit – thus, if they consume too much hair it could form a ball in the stomach and cause serious health problems.

For this reason, it is essential that you brush your rabbit at least once a week to remove loose and dead hairs from its coat. During shedding seasons, you may need to brush Lionhead Rabbits once a day or even multiple times a day to keep up.

d.) Other General Tips

In addition to vaccinating your rabbit you should also check its condition on your own from time to time. Take a look inside your rabbit's ears for signs of wax buildup or infection – unpleasant odor may also be a sign of infection. Your rabbit's feet should be dry and free from sores. If you notice patches of skin where the fur has worn away or swelling, you should seek immediate veterinary care.

When petting your rabbit, take the time to check its skin and coat. If you notice white flakes or tiny white dots, your rabbit could have mites or fleas. If you provide your rabbit with adequate chew toys, you shouldn't have to worry about its teeth becoming overgrown. You should, however, make frequent checks to see if the teeth are properly aligned – if they aren't, your rabbit could develop molar spurs or abscesses in the mouth.

The nails of Lionhead Rabbits grow continuously so you will need to trim them every six to eight weeks. Trimming your rabbit's nails is not a difficult task but it does require a degree of caution. Inside your rabbit's nail lies the quick – a vein which supplies blood to the nail. If you cut your rabbit's nails too short, you could sever the quick and induce severe bleeding. When clipping your rabbit's nails it is best to only cut off the pointed tip. To be safe, have your veterinarian show you how to properly trim a rabbit's nails before you try it yourself.

Chapter Ten: Common Mistakes Owners Make

If you are new to keeping rabbits, you are likely to make a few mistakes while you are learning the ropes. However, even experienced rabbit owners make mistakes now and then.

If you want to provide your Lionhead Rabbits with the best care possible, take the time to read about some of the common mistakes owners make so you can avoid making these same mistakes yourself.

a.) Keeping Lionhead Rabbits Alone

Lionhead Rabbits are naturally social animals so they prefer to be kept with others of their own kind. Inexperienced rabbit owners often make the mistake of assuming that it will be too much work to care for more than one rabbit. This is not true, however, because you can keep both rabbits in the same cage and offer them the same food. In fact, it will be easier for you in the long run because your rabbits will be able to keep each other company and they will not demand as much attention from you.

The biggest problem occurs when outdoor rabbits are kept in hutches by themselves. Keeping your rabbits outdoors means that they will receive less attention and may become lonely. For this reason, it is essential that outdoor rabbits be kept at minimum in pairs. If you need to keep the rabbits separate for some reason, you can install mesh dividers in the hutch so the rabbits can still see each other.

b.) Using the Wrong Bedding

Choosing the right type of bedding is especially important for Lionhead Rabbits. Because these rabbits have such long, dense fur certain kinds of beddingcan get stuck in their coats. For this reason, you should avoid using shavings as bedding. A better option is to use straw or hay. When purchasing bedding, be sure it is non-toxic and fresh – you should also shake off as much dust as possible before using the bedding in your rabbit cage.

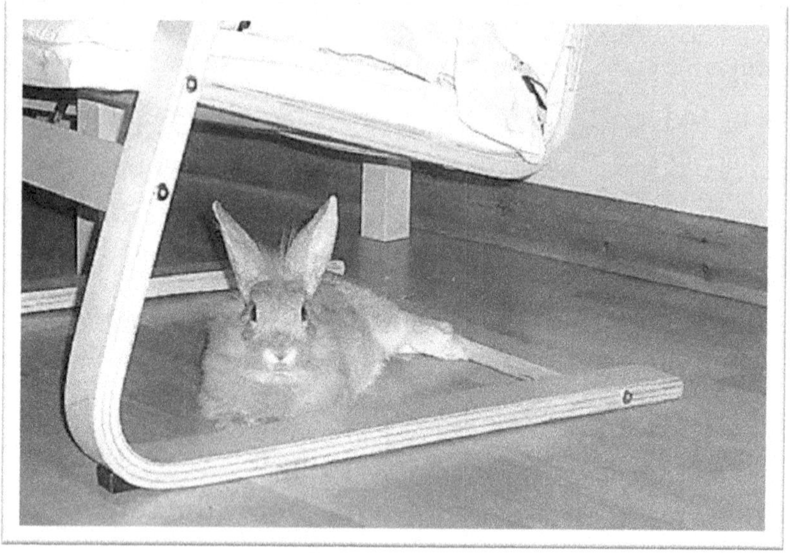

c.) Feeding the Wrong Food

The food you offer your Lionhead Rabbits has a direct impact on their health. You probably already understand the importance of eating the right foods for your own health, so it should be easy to see how the same is true of pet rabbits. Rabbits are herbivores by nature so they should be fed a plant based diet and not any animal-based foods.

The main component of a Lionhead Rabbit's diet should be grass hay like Timothy or meadow hay. You can also supplement your rabbit's diet with legume hay, fresh vegetables and commercial rabbit pellets. Do not assume that if you only give your rabbit commercial pellets he will be healthy – these pellets are not enough to give your rabbit the nutrition he requires.

Some rabbit owners also make the mistake of making changes in their rabbit's diet too quickly. Rabbits have very delicate digestive systems so any changes to their diets must be made slowly. Juvenile rabbits should not be fed vegetables while their digestive systems are still developing. Once they reach maturity, however, you can slowly begin introducing vegetables and then may offer them a variety of vegetables on a daily basis.

d.) Unwanted/Unexpected Breeding

Inexperienced rabbit owners sometimes fail to understand just how quickly and how often rabbits are capable of breeding. A female rabbit's estrus (heat) cycle is so frequent that she is almost continuously capable of getting pregnant. This is an important fact to keep in mind when keeping male and female rabbits in the same cage.

Many rabbit owners encounter unwanted breeding when they fail to separate the sexes early enough. Though female rabbits reach sexual maturity at 5 months of age and males at 6 months, they are capable of breeding as early as 3 months. To avoid unwanted breeding, it is essential that you separate the sexes before that point.

This is most likely to happen after a new litter is born. If you do not have experience keeping or breeding rabbits, you may not expect rabbits from the same litter to breed so readily. If you allow rabbits from the same litter to breed it can result in inbreeding and genetic defects. You shouldn't even keep male and female rabbits in the same cage if you want them to breed – outside a period of time long enough for them to mate, after which point the female should be removed from the cage.

Chapter Eleven: Frequently Asked Questions

Some of the Topics Covered in this Section Include:

General Care

Buying Lionhead Rabbits

Housing Lionhead Rabbits

Feeding Lionhead Rabbits

Breeding Lionhead Rabbits

Health Concerns

General Care

Q: *Should I buy one Lionhead Rabbit or two?*

A: The answer to this question has many variables. If you are a new rabbit owner, you may find it easier to care for one rabbit than to care for two. If you really think about it, however, caring for two rabbits is not a significant amount more work than caring for one – you can keep them both in the same cage and offer them the same food. You should also consider the fact that Lionhead Rabbits are friendly, social creatures and they enjoy the company of other rabbits. It is best to keep these rabbits in pairs or groups of three but they can be kept alone if provided with enough care and attention.

Q: *What kinds of costs should I be prepared for?*

A: Lionhead Rabbit owners are responsible for a number of costs, some of which recur on a monthly basis. When you are just getting started you will need to cover the costs for the rabbit cage and accessories as well as the rabbit itself. After setting up the cage and buying the rabbit, you will then need to purchase food and bedding on a monthly basis. You should also be prepared to cover additional costs occasionally for veterinary care and replacement items.

Q: *Can Lionhead Rabbits be kept outside?*

A: Pet rabbits can generally be kept outside in a hutch but you should think carefully before choosing this option. Rabbits that are kept outside are more likely to be exposed to disease and there is also the risk of predators getting into the cage and harming or killing your rabbits. Keeping your rabbits outdoors may also mean that you do not pay as much attention to them as you would if they were indoors – for this reason, it is essential that outdoor rabbits be kept in pairs or trios.

Buying Lionhead Rabbits

Q: *What precautions should I take when buying from a breeder?*

A: You should take the same precautions in buying from a breeder as you would in a pet store or shelter. You will need to examine the individual rabbits to make sure they are healthy before you even begin to talk about purchasing one. In addition to checking the health of the stock, you should also determine the breeder's experience and credentials. Ask the breeder questions to determine how much they know about the breed, how much experience they have and whether or not they have the required license or registration to breed rabbits legally.

Q: *Is it okay to buy Lionhead Rabbits from online ads?*

A: Purchasing any animals from an online ad is risky for a number of reasons. First, you will not be able to view the animal before purchase to make sure that it is in good condition. Second, by buying online means that the animal will have to be shipped. The shipping process can be extremely stressful and dangerous for animals because they may be exposed to extreme temperatures and rough handling. Please avoid buying animals online.

Q: *What are the benefits of adopting an adult rabbit?*

A: Many people prefer to buy baby rabbits because they want to raise the rabbit themselves. While this is a wonderful experience, there are also several unique benefits involved in adopting an adult rabbit. Adult rabbits are more likely to already be litter trained which will save you the hassle of having to do it yourself. It is also more likely that the rabbit will already be spayed or neutered because this is a policy most shelters enforce. Adopting an adult rabbit may also be a little cheaper than buying a baby rabbit from a pet store or breeder.

Housing Lionhead Rabbits

Q: *Can I build my own rabbit cage?*

A: Yes, you can build your own rabbit cage as long as you use the appropriate materials and make it the right size. The easiest way to make your own rabbit cage is to use stackable wire cubes to create a multi-level cage. Insert wooden dowels through the gaps to create supports for wooden shelves and line the shelves with towels to make them more comfortable for your rabbit.

Q: *Can I let my rabbit play outside?*

A: Yes, you can let your rabbit play outside as long as you take a few precautions. First, it is important that your rabbit receives all the necessary vaccinations to keep him protected against disease. Second, you should build or buy an outdoor rabbit run that will keep your rabbit safe while he is outside. Even while your rabbit is confined to the run you should keep an eye on him.

Q: *How big should my rabbit cage be?*

A: In response to this question, many experienced rabbit owners will reply "the bigger the better." At minimum, however, your rabbit cage should be wide enough for your rabbit to stretch all the way out. The cage should be about four times your rabbit's size in length. Keeping your rabbit in a cage too small can result in health problems.

Q: *How often should I clean my rabbit's cage?*

A: The best answer to this question is "as often as necessary". If you have multiple rabbits in one cage or one messy rabbit, you may need to clean out the cage more often than you would for a single rabbit. Generally, you should plan to change your rabbit's bedding once a week but you may need to clean the litter box two or three times within that same period of time.

Feeding Lionhead Rabbits

Q: *Are there any plants that are poisonous to rabbits?*

A: Yes. Please see Chapter Five under "Feeding Lionhead Rabbits" for more details.

Q: *Do I need to give my rabbit supplements?*

A: As long as you provide your Lionhead Rabbit with a healthy, varied diet you should not need to give them any supplements. Giving your rabbit supplements is, however, an option and it can help to boost their nutrition. One option is to provide your rabbit with a salt or mineral block. In addition to giving your rabbit iodine and other minerals, it can also help relieve their boredom. Small pieces of fruit such as banana or apple can be used as treats but should only be given occasionally. Do not give your rabbit any human food or vitamin supplements without checking with your veterinarian first.

Q: *Should I refill my rabbit's bowl of pellets during the day?*

A: No. If you keep refilling your rabbit's bowl, your rabbit may eat more of the pellets than hay. Hay and vegetables are the most important parts of your rabbit's daily diet so you should do what you can to encourage him to eat those foods. Commercial pellets are a supplement to your rabbit's diet of hay and vegetables. If unsure, your vet will be able to give you guidance.

Breeding Lionhead Rabbits

Q: *At what age can I begin breeding my Lionhead Rabbits?*

A: Female Lionhead rabbits are generally considered sexually mature at 5 months while males are considered sexually mature at 6 months.

Q: *Can't I just keep a male and female in the same cage together if I want to breed them?*

A: Keeping male and female rabbits together in the same cage will result in breeding, but it may not be a healthy situation for your rabbits. After a female rabbit becomes pregnant, she will enter a 31-day gestation period. During that time it is not possible for the female to become pregnant again but the male may continue to attempt to breed. This can be exhausting for the female rabbit and dangerous if the male becomes aggressive in his advances. It is best to separate the sexes after breeding to ensure that the female rabbit is able to rest and the babies develop properly.

Q: *Should I worry if the Dam doesn't begin feeding the babies right away?*

A: No. It is not uncommon for a Lionhead Rabbit Dam to wait a day or two before they begin feeding their young. If she has not begun feeding them after two days, however, you may want to consider using a foster mother. If you introduce the litter to a foster mother while they are young enough, she will be less likely to reject them.

Q: *Can I move the babies from the nest box to clean it?*

A: No. If you observe the female rabbit you will notice that she never moves the babies from the nest box. When Lionhead Rabbits are born they are virtually hairless so they depend on the nest box and their collective body heat to survive. If you move the baby rabbits from the nest box, they could die from exposure.

Q: *Will I need a license if I plan to breed my Lionhead Rabbits?*

A: The answer to this question varies depending where you live. In most cases, a license is not required for individuals to keep Lionhead Rabbits as pets. If you live in the United States and plan to breed your rabbits, however, you may need to obtain a license. A license is not required in the U.K. to breed rabbits. Be sure to check with your local council to find the answer to this question.

Health Concerns

Q: *What vaccinations are required for rabbits?*

A: Vaccinations are not required but certain ones are highly recommended. The two most important vaccines for rabbits are against myxomatosis and rabbit hemorrhagic disease (RHD). Both of these diseases are very serious and often fatal. Aside from preventive vaccination, treatments for these diseases are typically ineffective. Check with your veterinarian as the recommendations will vary from place to place.

Q: *Do I need to have my rabbit examined by a vet?*

A: Again, it is your choice whether or not you provide your rabbit with routine veterinary care. Some rabbit owners prefer to save themselves the expense of veterinary visits while others see the value in it. The benefit of taking your rabbit in for regular check-ups is that you can catch diseases and conditions in the early stages and provide treatment. You can also keep your rabbit up to date on recommended vaccinations.

Q: *What are the health benefits of spaying/neutering?*

A: Some rabbits exhibit behavioral changes if they are not spayed or neutered - they may become more aggressive and they may spray urine. For female rabbits, spaying greatly reduces the risk for uterine cancer. Uterine cancer is one of the most common causes of death in un-spayed rabbits and it is often untreatable by the time a diagnosis is made. Neutering male rabbits will help prevent them from fighting with other rabbits which could also serve to extend their lives.

Chapter Twelve: Relevant Websites

1.) Shopping

When you start looking around the internet it can take some time to track down exactly what you are looking for.

A one-stop shop for all your rabbit needs is what is required and the sites below offer you the convenience of pulling together many of the best products from around the web. Enjoy Shopping!

United States of America Website
www.rabbitsorbunnies.com

United Kingdom Website
www.rabbitsorbunnies.co.uk

2.) Food for Lionhead Rabbits

United States of America Websites:

"Nutrition of Rabbits." Merck Veterinary Manual. www.merckmanuals.com/vet/exotic_and_laboratory_animals/rabbits/nutrition_of_rabbits.html

"Feeding Rabbits." Raising-Rabbits.com. www.raising-rabbits.com/feeding-rabbits.html

"Caring for Your New Rabbit." King of the Jungle Rabbitry. kingofthejunglerabbitry.webs.com/rabbitcare.htm

United Kingdom Websites:

Millen, Dee. "Basic Dietary Guidelines for a Healthy Lionhead Rabbit." Dee Millen Rabbits. www.lionheadrabbit.co.uk/6.html

"A Healthy Diet for Rabbits." The Royal Society for the Prevention of Cruelty to Animals. www.rspca.org.uk/allaboutanimals/pets/rabbits/diet

3.) Care for Lionhead Rabbits

United States of America Websites:

Seja, Ledan. "Lionhead Bunny Facts." PawNation. animals.pawnation.com/lionhead-bunny-2058.html

"Lionhead Rabbit." CentralPets.com. centralpets.com/animals/mammals/rabbits/rbt1492.html

"Rabbit Cage, to Cage or Not to Cage?" PetRabbitInfo.com. www.petrabbitinfo.com/rabbitcage.html

"Cages and Supplies." Welsh's Honeybuns. www.welshrabbitry.com/lionheadvanodine.html

United Kingdom Websites:

"Housing of Rabbits." Merck Veterinary Manual. www.merckmanuals.com/vet/exotic_and_laboratory_animals/rabbits/housing_of_rabbits.html

"A Suitable Environment for Rabbits." The Royal Society for the Prevention of Cruelty to Animals. www.rspca.org.uk/allaboutanimals/pets/rabbits/environment

4.) Health Information for Lionhead Rabbits

United States of America Websites:

"Rabbit Health." Bunny Luv Rabbit Resource Center.
www.bunnyluv.org/#!rabbit-health/c511

"Health and Medical Issues." Welsh's Honeybuns.
www.welshrabbitry.com/health.html

"Lionhead Bunny." Pet Health and Care.
www.pethealthandcare.com/types-of-bunnies/lionhead-bunny.html

"Rabbit Diseases." Raising-Rabbits.com.
www.raising-rabbits.com/rabbit-diseases.html

United Kingdom Websites:

"Viral Diseases of Rabbits." Merck Veterinary Manual.
www.merckmanuals.com/vet/exotic_and_laboratory_animals/rabbits/viral_diseases_of_rabbits.html

"Lionhead." BunnyHugga.
www.bunnyhugga.com/a-to-z/breeds/lionhead.html

"Rabbit Health and Welfare." The Royal Society for the Prevention of Cruelty to Animals.
www.rspca.org.uk/allaboutanimals/pets/rabbits/health

5.) General Information for Lionhead Rabbits

United States of America Websites:

Parker, Lee. "Male Lionhead Bunny for a Pet." PawNation. animals.pawnation.com/male-lionhead-bunny-pet-1428.html

"Facts on Lionhead Rabbits." PetRabbitInfo.com. www.petrabbitinfo.com/lionheadrabbits.html

"Lionhead Rabbit FAQs." Welsh Rabbitry. www.welshrabbitry.com/rabbitfaq.html

"Housing of Rabbits." Merck Veterinary Manual. www.merckmanuals.com/vet/exotic_and_laboratory_animals/rabbits/housing_of_rabbits.html

United Kingdom Websites:

"Lionhead Colours." National Lionhead Rabbit Club. lionheadrabbit.info/lionhead-colours/index.html

"Thinking of Getting a Rabbit?" Surrey Lionhead Rabbits. surreylionheads.webs.com/info.htm

"Lionhead History." National Lionhead Rabbit Club. lionheadrabbit.info/lionhead-history.html

"Housing for Your Rabbit." Dee Millen Rabbits. www.lionheadrabbit.co.uk/7.html

6.) Showing Lionhead Rabbits

United States of America Websites:

Gibbons, Gail. "Visualization of the Lionhead Standard." The Lionheads of Cimmaron.
www.cimmarononline.com/LHvisual.htm

"The Lionhead Standard." North American Lionhead Rabbit Club.
www.lionhead.us/aboutlionheads/standards.htm

Gibbons, Gail. "Posing the Lionhead on the Show Table." The Lionheads of Cimmaron.
www.cimmarononline.com/LHposing.htm

"Showing Lionheads." Twilight Bunny Brewery.
"What to Expect at a Rabbit Show." Circus Lions Rabbitry.
www.circuslionsrabbitry.com/whattoexpectatrabbitshow.htm

United Kingdom Websites:

"Lionhead Standard." National Lionhead Rabbit Club.
lionheadrabbit.info/lionhead-standard.html

"Around the Shows." National Lionhead Rabbit Club.
www.lionheadrabbit.info/show.htm

"Lionhead Rabbits – Breed Standard." Dee Millen Rabbits.
www.deemillen.co.uk/lionhead_rabbits.php

Index

A

B

C

D

E

F

G

H

I

J

K

L

M

N

O

P

R

S

T

U

V

W

Photo Credits

Cover Design:- Liliana Gonzalez Garcia, ipublicidades.com (info@ipublicidades.com)

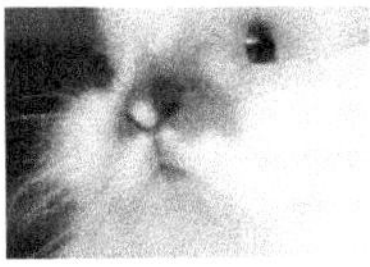

Photo by Flickr user David~O
www.flickr.com/photos/8106459@N07/4088173142

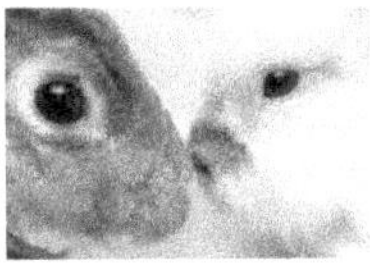

Photo by Flickr user David~O
www.flickr.com/photos/8106459@N07/4088173342

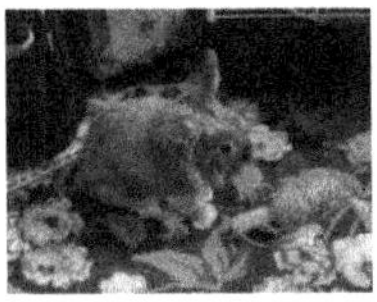

Photo by Flickr user Bunnygoth
www.flickr.com/photos/bunnygoth/8324964760

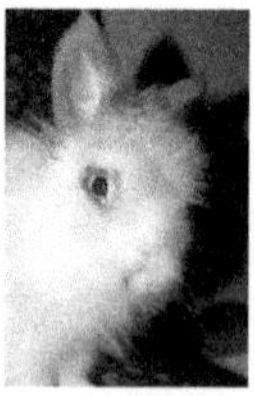

Photo by Milkman.gr

http://commons.wikimedia.org/wiki/File:LionHead_Bunny.jpg

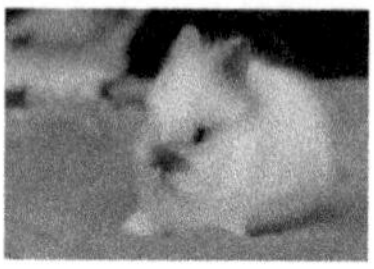

Photo by Flickr user David~O

www.flickr.com/photos/8106459@N07/4013449990

Photo by Chatsam

http://fr.m.wikipedia.org/wiki/Fichier:Lapin_nain_tete_de_lion.j
peg

Photo by RabbitPower

http://bg.wikipedia.org/wiki/%D0%A4%D0%B0%D0%B9%D0%B
B:Sir_the_first.jpg

Photo by Emmaima
http://commons.wikimedia.org/wiki/File:Lionhead_bunny.jpg

Photo by Flickr user Bunnygoth
www.flickr.com/photos/bunnygoth/8342776476

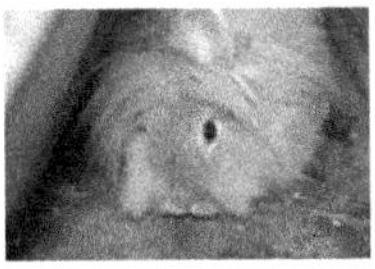

Photo by Flickr user Curtis.Kennington
www.flickr.com/photos/curtiskennington/3630326818

Photo by Flickr user Fantasya72
www.flickr.com/photos/33848626@N03/3152590837

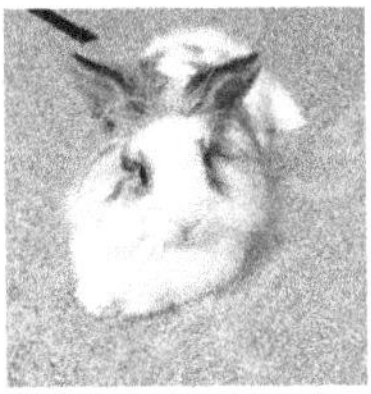

Photo by Caffeinegeek
http://en.m.wikipedia.org/wiki/File:White_Lionhead_Rabbit.jpg

Photo by Flickr user Myszka&Agnieszka

www.flickr.com/photos/77508660@N07/7001546346

Photo by Flickr user Myszka&Agnieszka

www.flickr.com/photos/77508660@N07/7350857156

Photo by Flickr user Kansas_City_Royalty

www.flickr.com/photos/kansas_city_royalty/460959478

Photo by Flickr user Ragnvaeig

www.flickr.com/photos/ragnvaeig/2854998960

Photo by Flickr user valeehill

www.flickr.com/photos/valeehill/5449080898

Photo by Flickr user ManeyDigital

www.flickr.com/photos/maneydigital/5428755573

Photo by Flickr user Kansas_City_Royalty

www.flickr.com/photos/kansas_city_royalty/460959496

Photo by Greg Hewgill (Flickr)

http://commons.wikimedia.org/wiki/File:Well_fed_rabbit.jpg

Photo by Flicks user CoalyBunny

www.flickr.com/photos/coaly/4841437520

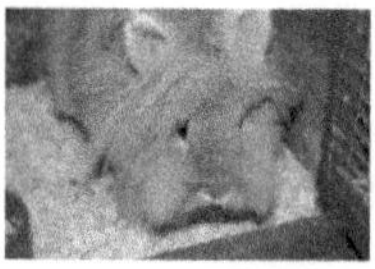

Photo by Flickr user Curtis.Kennington

www.flickr.com/photos/curtiskennington/3629536333

Photo by Sistercja (Own work)

http://commons.wikimedia.org/wiki/File:Lionhead_Rabbit.jpg

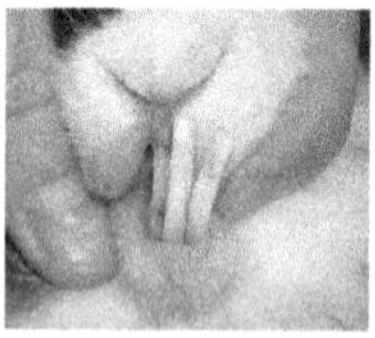

Photo by Uwe Gille

http://commons.wikimedia.org/wiki/File:Bradygnathia-superior-rabbit.jpg

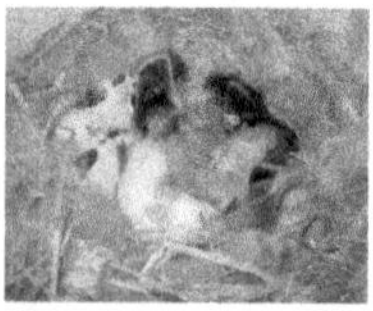

Photo by Flickr user Spigoo

www.flickr.com/photos/spigoo/2099086

Photo by Flickr user Cassicat4

www.flickr.com/photos/naturesauraphotography/4883809547

Photo by Linsenhejhej

http://commons.wikimedia.org/wiki/File:White_lionhead_rabbit.jpg

Photo by Flickr user Bunnygoth

www.flickr.com/photos/bunnygoth/6098563765

Photo by Calgirl2

http://en.wikipedia.org/wiki/File:Lionhead_rabbit.jpg

Photo by Sistercja

http://commons.wikimedia.org/wiki/File:Lionhead_Relax.jpg

Photo by Mmm Daffodils
http://commons.wikimedia.org/wiki/File%3APissed_Off_Raised_Rabbit.JPG

Photo by Flickr user DownattheZoo
www.flickr.com/photos/devolve/5422862813

Image courtesy www.rabbitsorbunnies.com/

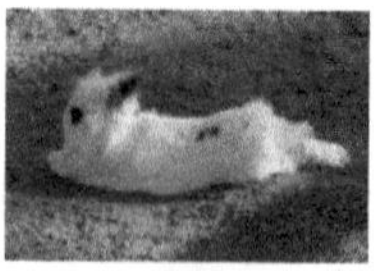

Photo by Flickr user David~O
www.flickr.com/photos/8106459@N07/4104376453

References

"A Healthy Diet for Rabbits." The Royal Society for the Prevention of Cruelty to Animals.
www.rspca.org.uk/allaboutanimals/pets/rabbits/diet

"Alleviate Rabbit Boredom with Interactive Toys." Drs. Foster and Smith.
www.drsfostersmith.com/pic/article.cfm?aid=778

"A Suitable Environment for Rabbits." The Royal Society for the Prevention of Cruelty to Animals.
www.rspca.org.uk/allaboutanimals/pets/rabbits/environment

"Around the Shows." National Lionhead Rabbit Club.
www.lionheadrabbit.info/show.htm

"Breeding Rabbits." DebMark Rabbit Education Resource.
www.debmark.com/rabbits/breeding.htmhttp://www.debmar

"Bunny Care." Tranquility Trail Animal Sanctuary.
http://tranquilitytrail.org/RabbitCare.html

"Cages and Supplies." Welsh's Honeybuns.
www.welshrabbitry.com/lionheadvanodine.html

"Can I Have a Pet Rabbit?" Department of Agriculture, Fisheries and Forestry Biosecurity Queensland.
www.daff.qld.gov.au/documents/Biosecurity_EnvironmentalPests/IPA-Keeping-Rabbits-As-Pets-PA15.pdf

"Caring for Your New Rabbit." King of the Jungle Rabbitry.
http://kingofthejunglerabbitry.webs.com/rabbitcare.htm

"Children and Pet Rabbits." My House Rabbit. www.myhouserabbit.com/tip_children.php

Doering, Laura. "Rabbits and Other Pets." Small Animal Channel. www.smallanimalchannel.com/rabbits/rabbit-interaction/rabbits-and-pets.aspx

"Facts on Lionhead Rabbits." PetRabbitInfo.com. www.petrabbitinfo.com/lionheadrabbits.html

"Feeding Rabbits." Raising-Rabbits.com. www.raising-rabbits.com/feeding-rabbits.html

Gibbons, Gail. "Posing the Lionhead on the Show Table." The Lionheads of Cimmaron. www.cimmarononline.com/LHposing.htm

Gibbons, Gail. "Visualization of the Lionhead Standard." The Lionheads of Cimmaron. www.cimmarononline.com/LHvisual.htm

"Health and Medical Issues." Welsh's Honeybuns. www.welshrabbitry.com/health.html

"History – How it All Started." National Lionhead Rabbit Club. www.lionheadrabbit.info/history.htm

"Housing of Rabbits." Merck Veterinary Manual. www.merckmanuals.com/vet/exotic_and_laboratory_animals/rabbits/housing_of_rabbits.html

"Housing for Your Rabbit." Dee Millen Rabbits. www.lionheadrabbit.co.uk/7.html

"Housing Options for Your Pet Rabbit." House Rabbit Network. www.rabbitnetwork.org/articles/houses.shtml

"How to Build an Indoor Bunny Cage" BreyFamily.net. http://breyfamily.net/bunnycage.html

"How to Get a Healthy Bunny." Circus Lions Rabbitry. www.circuslionsrabbitry.com/gettingahealthybunny.htm

Krempels, Dana. "Spay or Neuter my Rabbit?" Miami University. www.bio.miami.edu/hare/spay.html

"Licensing and Registration Under the Animal Welfare Act." Animal and Plant Health Inspection Service. www.aphis.usda.gov/animal_welfare/downloads/aw/awlicreg.pdf

"Lionhead." BunnyHugga. www.bunnyhugga.com/a-to-z/breeds/lionhead.html

"Lionhead Bunny." Pet Health and Care. www.pethealthandcare.com/types-of-bunnies/lionhead-bunny.html

"Lionhead Colours." National Lionhead Rabbit Club. http://lionheadrabbit.info/lionhead-colours/index.html

"Lionhead History." National Lionhead Rabbit Club. http://lionheadrabbit.info/lionhead-history.html

"Lionhead Mane and Coat Development Pictorial." Circus Lions Rabbitry. www.circuslionsrabbitry.com/lionheadrabbitmanes.htm

"Lionhead Rabbit." CentralPets.com. http://centralpets.com/animals/mammals/rabbits/rbt1492.html

"Lionhead Rabbit FAQs." Welsh Rabbitry. www.welshrabbitry.com/rabbitfaq.html

"Lionhead Rabbits – Breed Standard." Dee Millen Rabbits. www.deemillen.co.uk/lionhead_rabbits.php

"Lionhead Standard." National Lionhead Rabbit Club. http://lionheadrabbit.info/lionhead-standard.html

Millen, Dee. "Basic Dietary Guidelines for a Healthy Lionhead Rabbit." Dee Millen Rabbits. www.lionheadrabbit.co.uk/6.html

"Nutrition of Rabbits." Merck Veterinary Manual. www.merckmanuals.com/vet/exotic_and_laboratory_animals/rabbits/nutrition_of_rabbits.html

"Outdoor Rabbit Housing." The Rabbit House. www.therabbithouse.com/outdoor/

Parker, Lee. "Male Lionhead Bunny for a Pet." PawNation. http://animals.pawnation.com/male-lionhead-bunny-pet-1428.html

"Rabbit Cage, to Cage or Not to Cage?" PetRabbitInfo.com. www.petrabbitinfo.com/rabbitcage.html

"Rabbit Color Chart." Roaring Heights Rabbitry. www.roaringheights.com/rabbitcolorchart.htm

"Rabbit Health." Bunny Luv Rabbit Resource Center. www.bunnyluv.org/#!rabbit-health/c511

"Rabbit Health and Welfare." The Royal Society for the Prevention of Cruelty to Animals. www.rspca.org.uk/allaboutanimals/pets/rabbits/health

"Rabbit Diseases." Raising-Rabbits.com. www.raising-rabbits.com/rabbit-diseases.html

"Rabbit Legislation Section." Rabbit Educational Society. http://rabbitedsociety.webs.com/legislation.htm

"Rabbits and Vegetables." The Humane Society of the United States. www.humanesociety.org/animals/rabbits/tips/rabbit_vegetables.html

"Rabbit Vaccinations." The Royal Society for the Prevention of Cruelty to Animals. www.rspca.org.uk/allaboutanimals/pets/rabbits/health/vaccinationshttp://www.rspca.org.uk/allaboutanim

Seja, Ledan. "Lionhead Bunny Facts." PawNation. http://animals.pawnation.com/lionhead-bunny-2058.html

"Showing Lionheads." Twilight Bunny Brewery.

Smith, Kathy. "The Basics of Litterbox Training." House Rabbit Network. www.rabbitnetwork.org/articles/litter.shtml

Smith, P.A. "Spaying or Neutering Your Pet Bunny." My House Rabbit. www.myhouserabbit.com/tip_spayneuter.php

"Spaying and Neutering." House Rabbit Society. http://rabbit.org/faq-spaying-and-neutering/

"The Beginning." The British Rabbit Council. www.thebrc.org/history.htm

"The Bunny – From Conception to Weaning." DebMark Rabbit Education Resource. www.debmark.com/rabbits/bunnies.htm

"The Lionhead Standard." North American Lionhead Rabbit Club.
www.lionhead.us/aboutlionheads/standards.htm

"The Time and Costs Involved in Keeping Rabbits." RSPCA.org.uk.
www.rspca.org.uk/ImageLocator/LocateAsset?asset=document&assetId=1232729413756&mode=prd

"Thinking of Getting a Rabbit?" Surrey Lionhead Rabbits.
http://surreylionheads.webs.com/info.htm

"Toxic Plants." Rabbit Advocates.
www.adoptarabbit.com/articles/toxic.html#b

"Viral Diseases of Rabbits." Merck Veterinary Manual.
www.merckmanuals.com/vet/exotic_and_laboratory_animals/rabbits/viral_diseases_of_rabbits.html

"What to Expect at a Rabbit Show." Circus Lions Rabbitry.
www.circuslionsrabbitry.com/whattoexpectatrabbitshow.htm

"Zoning and Rabbits." Rabbit Education Society.
http://rabbitedsociety.webs.com/zoning.htm

CPSIA information can be obtained
at www.ICGtesting.com
Printed in the USA
JSHW042019120123
36148JS00008BA/915

9 781909 820012